SOUTHWESTERN INDIAN POTTERY

Text and Photography by Bruce Hucko

Bruce Hucko is an independent photographer, author, educator, and children's art coach who lives in Moab, Utah. The primary theme in all of his work is the relationship among community, art, landscape, and people. Bruce taught art and photography on the Navajo Reservation and among the northern Pueblos, creating two national award-winning books of children's art.

· His photography appears in national publications and is widely collected. Working in both color and black-and-white, he produces fine art prints, assignment work, and special projects. Bruce is the primary photographer for KC Publications' Southwestern Indian Arts and Crafts Series. He also photographed *Santa Fe Trail: Voyage of Discovery*.

Special Thanks to the artists and the following institutions for their help: Andrea Fisher Fine Pottery, Arizona State Museum, Bahti Indian Arts, Chimayo Trading Post, Nancy Dahl (private collection), Elvis Torres Gallery, Rio Grande Trading Company, School of American Research, and Wheelwright Museum.

INDEX

*Southwest Indian pottery
emerged from an ancient land and people.
First produced out of the necessity
to hold water, cook, and store grain,
it has evolved into a refined and
coveted art form. In each piece
can be seen and felt a strong
connection to the land—
the timeless beauty of the pottery makers.*

The Wonderful World of Pottery

The pottery tradition among American Indian tribes in the southwest United States is nearly 2,000 years old. The ancient cultures who made pottery and their modern descendants share a foundation rooted deep in the land. Known in modern terms as the Anasazi, Hohokam, and Mogollon, the first pottery cultures of the Southwest gave rise to unique pottery traditions among their descendants—the Pueblo, Hopi, Navajo, Tohono O'odham, and other Native groups. Common among all of these people is the belief that Earth is the Mother of the people. This belief is stated in many ceremonial prayers and songs, regular conversation, and the arts. In its most fundamental state, the pottery tradition of the Southwest can be seen as a physical extension of the Mother-Earth relationship.

Pottery materials—clay, sand, wood for firing and vegetal or mineral paints for decoration—are viewed as gifts from Mother Earth. Prayers are offered during collecting, building, and firing. The pottery-making process is very intimate and time-consuming, and as a result many potters speak of their final pottery pieces as their "children."

Just as pottery pieces can be seen as an extension of the family, so does the making of pottery require family involvement. A grandmother's design shared by the mother may be placed on a vessel made by the artist whose children and spouse helped gather and process the clay that

Handcrafted mostly of earthen materi
each piece of Southwest Indian pott
is imbued with the artist's creative sp
Each piece connects the traditio
culture of the artist with that of
collector in a meaningful w
The hands on the central pi
by Hopi potter Steve Lu
serve as a metaphor
creation and understand
across cultural differenc

Archaeologists tell us that pottery was firs
made primarily for functional reasons.
In this Mesa Verde style black-on-white p
dated to about A.D. 1250 and excavated
by Crow Canyon Archaeological Center,
we see an expression of artistic merit. Its
painted design is often seen repeated
in contemporary work, suggesting a continu
of understanding and meaning.

Southwestern Indian pottery is the center of many families' cultural and economic livelihood. The work that goes into each piece is arduous, time-consuming, and carefully considered. A single piece may involve months of work. This photograph shows the basic process of building a clay pot. (Please see pages 31-33 for a detailed discussion of the process.) (from bottom left) Raw clay is gathered and prepared. The pot is formed using coil and pinch techniques. The rough shape is sanded into the desired form. This piece was then carved. Prior to firing, the pot is polished using a natural clay slip and smooth stone. The piece was fired black in an outdoor reduction fire.

was hauled in an uncle's borrowed truck and that was fired using wood donated by a cousin. When you purchase any piece of pottery handmade in the Southwest, you are supporting the sanctity of family and the continuation and flowering of Native culture.

In this new century we honor those families and individuals who helped to create, maintain, and encourage the pottery tradition. We also welcome those families and individuals who will foster new generations of clay artists, bringing forth the best of traditions while pursuing new forms of creative self-expression within the changing, versatile, beautiful medium of clay.

ANCESTRAL BEGINNINGS

The pottery tradition in the Southwest is as diverse as the Native people who inhabit it. The region encompasses nearly all of the state of Arizona, southern Utah, the southwest corner of Colorado, the lands west of the Pecos River in New Mexico, and northern parts of Mexico.

The range of topography, ecology, and climate that exists here is so extreme as to make human habitation nearly impossible. Yet in prehistoric times, all of these lands were inhabited by hunter-gatherer people. The Paleo-Indian cultures and succeeding Archaic cultures roamed the Southwest from at least 12,000 B.C. to 1500 B.C.

The adaptation to corn-based agriculture (approximately 500 B.C.) dramatically altered the development and life-style of desert people. No longer having to only hunt and gather food, these early people began to settle into specific regions and develop unique cultures. The Hohokam, Mogollon, Anasazi (now called Ancestral Puebloan), and several other groups emerged from these lands to form the primary cultures responsible for today's pottery traditions.

Initially, though, there was no pottery, nor masonry buildings. These bands of early farmers were wandering on the open land and storing their food in woven containers. As these early cultures became more dependent upon farming, better methods were devised for storing increasing amounts of food. At first, shallow pits lined with slab stones, called cists, were employed.

Patterns of development and modern dating techniques suggest that pottery first appeared in the southern Southwest, possibly among the Hohokam, and migrated northward with other forms of knowledge as bands of people made contact to trade. The earliest pottery is quite well made, suggesting it was learned from without rather than developing independently in this region. Whatever the process, by approximately A.D. 400, the making and use of pottery had established itself in the Southwest.

From its earliest adaptation pottery has proven to be an important contribution to cultural development in the Southwest. Combined with farming, pottery nurtured a more sedentary life-style which, in turn, created an environment for the development of trade, ceremonialism, art, and architecture. Pottery remains, due to their profusion and longevity, offer archaeologists clues to trade patterns, population, transfer of knowledge, and the advancement of technology among early cultures.

Archaeologists dig, date, categorize, and study ancient pottery in order to derive information about past cultures. The physical location of whole pots and shards, their style, and their composition can tell us much about ancient trade patterns, population, building techniques, and lifeways. All of this information is lost if someone removes the pots from their settings. The corrugated pot above was found and left in situ. The one below was first excavated by Richard Wetherill in the 1890s and rediscovered in its current museum home by the Wetherill-Grand Gulch Research Project, which traces historic collections in hopes of being able to reconnect ancient artifacts with their original landscape context. Both convey the technical proficiency and artistry of their makers.

CONNECTIONS PAST AND PRESENT

The pottery of ancient times may have created the techniques, basic designs, and forms of modern work, but no one could have imagined the great profusion of creative expression that is currently being shown by and is growing among clay artists. Today we are witnessing an explosion of talent among the pottery-producing areas of the Southwest. As greater interest is shown by collectors, galleries, and museums in these works, new traditions are being formed. These new traditions are inexorably linked to the past in several meaningful ways.

This collection of seed pots illustrates the movement from function to art. The older, large piece dates from the 1870s and was used to store seeds for planting. Borrowing the concept, contemporary potters build miniature seed pots with elaborate designs and decorations. The opening, often much too small for a seed, allows the hot gases formed inside the pot during firing to escape. (Top left down to right) Rachel Concho, Rebecca Lucario, Joseph Lonewolf, Marie Suazo, Carolyn Concho

"Wedding" vases are produced in most pottery communities. These double-spouted forms have been used recently in some marriage ceremonies, ritually representing the male and female coming together as one. In a larger context, they also represent the marriage of mind and spirit, culture and creativity, people and earth that come together as one to form each piece of pottery. (Clockwise spiral from top left) Silas Claw, Elva Nampeyo, Elizabeth Manygoats, Celestina Tafoya, Lorenzo Spencer, Nellie V. Garcia, Linda Askan, Rita Malie, Jackie H. Shutiva, Yolanda Trujillo

Potters today often refer to the designs and shapes of their ancestors. Even child potters know where their talent, in part, comes from.

Many potters grind old potsherds into their clay to use as temper. At Hopi, for instance, the pottery remains from the village of Sikyatki are gathered, ground, and mixed into the clay as temper. One could say that the spirit of the old gives life to the new.

Old designs are also gathered, studied, and used in making new designs. Museums such as the School of American Research in Santa Fe, New Mexico, house great collections of ancient and historical pottery. Here, in archival vaults, potters from many traditions can come and study what has gone on before. Here, they can touch the hands of their ancestors.

The ancestors probably never imagined that an entire economy would form around the clay they were forming into a useful household tool. The development of pottery as a commercial, income-generating, artful enterprise began with changes in American life-style and technology. The railroad brought a "rediscovery" of Indian people by tourists from the coasts and Europe who wanted to buy things that "looked Indian." In 1922, the first Indian Market was held in Santa Fe, New Mexico, to foster quality and introduce the world to Pueblo arts. In Arizona, Hopi pottery was being marketed as "art pottery" instead of a functional ceramic.

Perhaps more than any other medium, pottery reflects the culture of its maker. Today's pottery is more innovative and diverse than ever before, and stands as a testament to the strength of tribal culture and the individual's creative self-expression.

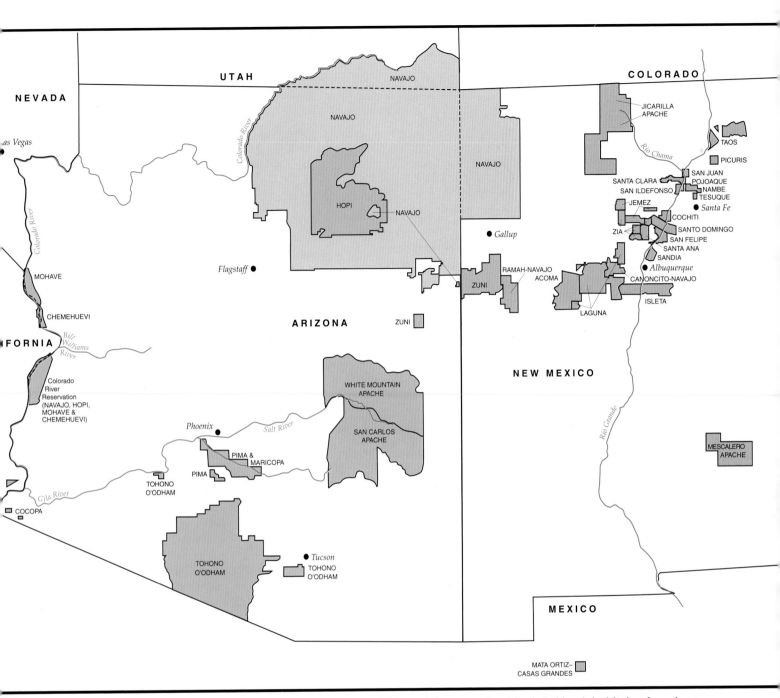

POTTERY COMMUNITIES

Practically every indigenous culture in the historic Southwest has a pottery tradition. Some have developed into a much-sought-after fine art while others struggle for acknowledgment. Some pottery traditions seem to be fading out while others are undergoing a rebirth.

The 19 pueblos of New Mexico and the Hopi in Arizona each have their own distinctive pottery style. The Navajo have a simple, yet elegant pottery tradition. The Tohono O'odham, Maricopa, and Apache also create unique and expressive forms. The people of Mata Ortiz, Mexico, have recently invented a dynamic tradition. Pottery is very much alive, and the communities who create it seem to be growing numerically and creatively.

Thirty-eight sovereign tribal entities inhabit the American Southwest. Their traditional lands once stretched across the states of Arizona and New Mexico, the southern parts of California, Nevada, and Utah, southwestern Colorado, and northern Mexico. Each of the great ancient cultures of this landscape—the Anasazi, Hohokam, and Mogollon-Mimbres—had a pottery tradition. They migrated and changed becoming most of today's pottery-producing communities. The Navajo and Apache entered the area in historic times and developed their own style. Within the creative landscape of Southwest pottery, individual artists carry on a tradition that is hundreds and thousands of years old. They do so with a marked degree of personal and cultural expression. In making pottery they bring to life a connection with the land that has given them, their ancestors, and their descendants a rich and honorable life.

Santa Clara

The pueblo of Santa Clara is best known for its highly polished black- and redware. Pottery is traditionally carved or plain and formed into bowls, plates, wedding vases, and figurines. Contemporary artists, inspired by tradition, are exploring new forms and ways of decorating pottery. Multiple and spot-firings to alter and add color, asymmetrical pottery openings, and the use of silver and turquoise inlay are among the innovations found in Santa Clara pottery.

While most Pueblo pottery tends to be small, Santa Clara is also known to have produced large ollas, containers for water and food that exceeded two feet in height. Few Santa Clara potters make such large vessels today.

Research supports claims that carved pottery was begun by Margaret Tafoya and her mother SaraFina Gutierrrez Tafoya in the late 1920s. It is a tradition that has spawned many diverse approaches. Bold designs—including kiva steps, clouds, and a stylized bear paw that is associated only with Santa Clara—are carved deeply into the dry clay before firing.

Also common to contemporary Santa Clara is polychrome pottery. Potters use several colors

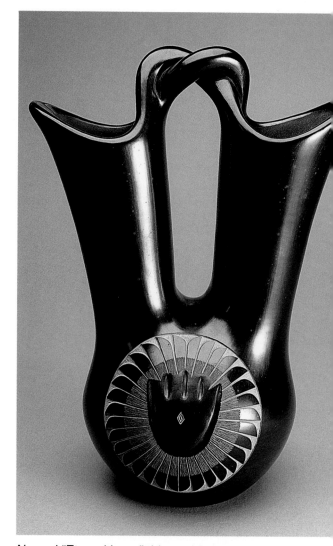

Named "Eternal Love," this wedding vase was designed for a mature couple. According to the artists, Judith and Andrew Harvier, the eagle-feather pattern represent the teachings of the Creator Spirit, and the bear paw— a common element on Santa Clara pottery—speaks to strength and reciprocity.

of clay slips to emphasize areas of decoration Wedding vases, tall double-spouted vessels, have been made in this manner since the early 1900s.

Where there is a strong pottery tradition there is usually a single family matriarch who began that tradition and infused a love and respect for it in all her descendants. Living potters in any one family may extend to three or more generations. By example, the family tree of SaraFina and Geronimo Tafoya shows over 75 working clay artists.

Santa Clara is home to two important contributions to the art of pottery. Miniature pottery forms, often less than two inches tall or one inch in diameter, and decorated with elaborate painted and etched designs, were "re-invented" here. Sometimes found in the ruins of pre-Columbian pueblos, their reintroduction as fine art is attributed to the Camilio "Sunflower" Tafoya family and

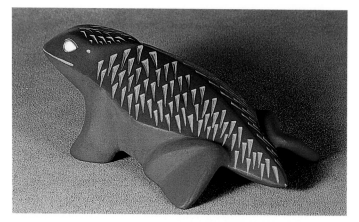

Animal figures are common among Santa Clara potters. Some, like the bear, have deep cultural significance. Others, like this horned lizard, are based on more whimsical ideas. Rather than selling for cash, potter Andrew Harvier traded this piece for a big-screen TV!

Santa Clara is well known for its red clay pots. The intense color is a combination of the clay and slip used, and proper firing. Color variations are subtle, ranging from a bright to brownish red. Potters carefully vary the elements to get just the color they want. Santa Clara pottery is generally thick, allowing for traditional deep-carved designs. Redware is the result of an open fire, where wood- and manure-fueled flames burn until they extinguish themselves. Tina Garcia, Marie Suazo, Madeline Tafoya

Miniatures bear all the markings, meanings, and processes of larger pottery. Standing from one to four inches in height, they are built as pinch pots, where small amounts of clay are pressed between the fingers to make the form. Once dried and sanded, and usually after firing, miniatures are decorated using the modern sgraffito method. Tools ranging from X-acto® knives to dental and laser implements are used to remove tiny amounts of surface clay, creating intricate patterns. (Clockwise from upper left) Debra Trujillo-Duwyenie, Emily Tafoya, Debra Trujillo-Duwyenie, Geri Naranjo (2), Delores Curran, Emily Tafoya, Delores Curran

was made famous by son Joseph Lonewolf. As the story is told, Camilio was teaching pottery to his children and in-laws in the early 1960s. The children, now among the finest potters anywhere, began making miniature animals. Today's miniatures evolved from the creative conversations held around the family kitchen table while everyone was potting.

The designs used are often from Santa Clara's storytelling tradition. Images depicting animals (butterflies, deer), Pueblo dancers, Mimbres pottery designs, nature scenes, and personal experiences abound.

Miniatures are now common in all pottery-producing areas.

The second contribution is intellectual. In many Santa Clara pottery families, there can be found a marked creative deviation from the norm. Whereas some communities observe rather conservative limitations on pottery forms and designs, Santa Clara seems to encourage artistic license. Cultural connections are exquisitely expressed in forms that stretch the outer limits of tradition and self-expression.

Santa Clara is located north of Santa Fe at the eastern edge of the Jemez Mountains and below the ancestral Puye' cliff dwellings. With more than 200 working potters, it is a haven of experimentation, quality, and sheer output. The range and sophistication of pottery made at Santa Clara is hard to match.

Deep-carved black pottery is the foundation of traditional Santa Clara pottery and remains a favorite of serious collectors. Many new potters seek to emulate the styles made popular by pottery matriarchs of the Tafoya and Naranjo families, while others explore new directions. (Clockwise from upper left) Teresita Naranjo, Jennie Trammel, Elizabeth Naranjo, Mela Youngblood, Elizabeth Naranjo

The descendants of Camilio Tafoya may make the most minis of any pottery family group. Styles and content reflect a variety of changing personal interests. Where grandfather Camilio would portray Indian dances, his son Joseph Lonewolf became famous for intricate portraits of wildlife. His granddaughter Rosemary creates highly personalized family travel and political scenes. This single family has helped the miniature style to flower. Joseph Lonewolf, Camilio Tafoya, Susan Romero, Greg Lonewolf, Grace Medicine Flower

San Ildefonso

The Tewa-speaking people of San Ildefonso trace their heritage back in time to the occupants of Bandelier, New Mexico, the Four Corners region, and the great ancient pueblos of Mesa Verde National Park.

Nestled between the Jemez and Sangre de Cristo mountains, 25 miles north of Santa Fe and next to the Rio Grande River, this small pueblo hosts one of the great pottery traditions of the Southwest.

San Ildefonso's pottery has become synonymous with Maria Martinez, possibly the best-known Pueblo potter in the world, made famous by her use of the black-on-black technique that she and her husband Julian first developed around 1919 with help and encouragement from the Museum of New Mexico. As a result, Maria and the black pottery became world famous and

Many potters employ personal feelings about a wide variety of subjects in their work. By including the fish in the body of the bear, Russell Sanchez may have been commenting on the reciprocal nature of life. Like any great work of art, the true meaning lies in the mind of the beholder.

San Ildefonso pottery is more than the classic black-on-black. While you can find "Maria-like" pottery in many shops, most of today's potters strive for individuality while maintaining a respect for traditional forms. Stew bowls, ollas, and plates have given way to lidded jars, figurines, and pots with asymmetrical openings rendered in redware, polychrome, and multi-tone variations. The positive environment of this small pueblo creates a healthy sense of competition among potters. Plate - Martha and Eric Fender; second row - Geraldine Gutierrez (2), Tse-Pe, Eric Fender; front - Adelphia Martinez, Geraldine Gutierrez, Becky Martinez

Nature is the potter's art supply store. The raw clays, sand temper, clay slip, most scrapers, polishing stones, wood and manure for firing, even the inspiration for forms and designs come from the earth. Elvis Torres shares his thoughts: "Before I can make pottery, I must clear my head and heart to only have positive thoughts. And I have to have some mellow rock, country, or symphonic music on to settle me down. When I form a pot on the puki (form for starting the base), I think of our ancestors who made pottery—especially my great-grandmother, because my puki was hers. I also listen to the clay because it will tell you what shape it wants to be and what painted designs will work best on it. I think we potters are fortunate to create with our hands what Mother Nature has given us."

brought an international market to the pueblo's doorstep that has become the foundation of their economy to this day.

Though small in population, San Ildefonso may have more potters per capita than any other pueblo. As a result, a great amount of creative diversity exists among its clay artists. Although Maria's technique of matte-painted, black-on-

The Avanyu, or water serpent, is often carved, painted, and incised onto pottery. Though the design varies by artist, each artist recognizes Avanyu as the guardian of springs, lakes, and rivers, making the serpent a revered form among the desert-dwelling Pueblo people. Jennifer S. Tse-Pe

black pottery is widely replicated by artists within the pueblo, San Ildefonso potters employ other styles of pottery which are equally beautiful.

Prior to black-on-black, San Ildefonso pottery was typically black and red on white. Two-tone black and sienna colored pottery was first developed by Maria's son Popovi Da. Such multi-coloring is now widespread among many pueblos. A number of potters here inlay small bits of shaped turquoise on pot surfaces, using them as a focal point for painted, carved, or etched designs.

Designs also vary widely. Traditionally, San Ildefonso pottery is recognized by use of the *Avanyu*, or water serpent, and the symmetrical, repeated feather motif of prehistoric origin. Other designs, abstract to the average viewer, are read by the artists as clouds (meeting, waving, standing, passing, etc.), rain, kiva steps, birds, and plants. Other potters have taken more personal approaches to their pottery by creating new shapes and designs and employing new colors of clay.

A visit to San Ildefonso can be very rewarding for it is only here where you can feel, taste, touch, hear, and even see how the pottery

Innovation and tradition come together on this pot by Russell Sanchez. The traditional feather pattern that encircles the pot represents the eagle, a bird held sacred by most Indian people. Imbedded in this work are heishe shell beads, probably traded or purchased from another pueblo. The addition of shell, silver, or special stones to pottery is gaining in popularity.

is made. Numerous artist-owned shops encircle the two dance plazas highlighted by San Ildefonso's historic round kiva. A stop at the pueblo-operated visitor center can direct you to more shops and specific artists. More importantly, a visit to the pueblo allows you to witness the community context out of which the pottery comes. If you plan well, you can visit San Ildefonso or many of the other pueblos on a dance or feast day and participate in the strong spiritual connection to the Earth that permeates the lives of all Indian artists.

Prior to the advent of black-on-black pottery, San Ildefonso made functional polychrome ollas, stew bowls, and other shapes. So important were they to the pueblo that they were called the same name as the pueblo—po-woh-ge, or "where the water cuts down through." As the new work of Maria gained fame, the making of polychrome diminished. Today there is a revival of the polychrome style. Potters like Eric Fender (middle right) are remaking traditional forms and exploring new forms with great artistic license. All other pieces are pre-1940 historic and unsigned.

15

Maria's Legacy

Perhaps nowhere else has one person so influenced the art of pottery making—including the influence on family—as has Maria Martinez.

In most pueblos, pottery means family. Maria was not alone in making her pottery. She built, her husband painted, and other family members occasionally contributed rough pots or other materials. Maria was generous with her knowledge, sharing her technique with any pueblo member who wanted to learn. Though awarded many prizes, international accolades, and monetary gain, she chose to keep her family home in the modesty of the pueblo. Her descendants practice that way of life even today. The family of Maria

Maria's technique calls for first painting a design using clay paint over a stone-polished red pot. The pottery is then fired in a reduction fire achieved by smothering the open fire with horse manure. The carbon contained within the sealed fire mound bonds with iron oxide in the clay, turning it black. The result is a matte-black design on a highly polished black pot. Maria pots are prized and highly sought after, often commanding 5,000- to 20,000-dollar-plus price tags. Hers were among the first pots to be signed, attesting to the commercial significance of her work. Signatures range from "Maria" to "Maria and Julian" (her husband) and "Maria and Santana" (her daughter-in-law). All pots by Maria Martinez

Martinez is a living legacy and a superb example of how the tradition is learned and passed on, creating "generations in clay."

Maria and Julian's children, Adam (and his wife Santana) and Popovi Da are noted potters. Popovi Da and his wife had one son, Tony Da, who became a marvelous painter and potter. He is said to be the first potter in the area to inset turquoise and other stones in his pottery designs.

Adam and Santana raised two children whose children have all become great potters in their own right and have given birth to many families of independent and creative potters.

For example, Barbara Gonzales, daughter of Adam and Santana's daughter Anita, is one of four great-grandchildren of Maria and Julian Martinez. Her four sons—Cavan, Aaron, Brandon, and Derek—all work in clay, and each has developed his own unique style and technique. Aaron's son, Jeramy, a great-great-great-grandchild of Maria and Julian, began working in clay as a baby and sold his first piece—a telephone made of a flattened ball of clay with finger-punched dial marks and a small coil of clay for a receiver—when he was three years old.

Families are strengthened through a bond with pottery, and the pottery tradition is also strengthened as families pass that heritage to future generations. Though family members may pursue other careers out of economic or personal interest, each knows that there is a warm and creatively nurturing family to come home to. In the work of the present, you can see continuity with the past and the future.

This "family portrait" shows the range of Maria's influence across four generations. (Clockwise from top left) A contemporary polychrome by Cavan Gonzales (great-great-grandson). An incised redware by Tony Da (grandson). A traditional plain black vase by Adam (son) and Santana. Modern black-on-black Avanyu by Marvin Martinez (great-grandson). Seed pot with characteristic spider-web design by Barbara Gonzales (great-granddaughter). Lidded jar by Anita Martinez (granddaughter).

Brandon (right) and Derek Gonzales are great-great-grandsons of Maria. They have been taught by their mother Barbara to carry on the family tradition. "She helps me when I think of her," says Derek of Maria. The boys sell their work in the family-owned Sunbeam Gallery, with profits going towards their future education, family needs, and the occasional hamburger. It is clear from watching them that the family that clays together stays together.

Taos and Picuris

The northernmost pueblos of Taos and Picuris share a pottery tradition based in the creation of micaceous vessels. Since historic times potters have made bean pots and other functional shapes. Simple handles and lids are often added to increase the utility. Although some artists decorate their work with appliqué and incising, the finished piece is intended to work on a fire or stove in preference to metal pots for cooking beans and other food. Artists in both of these Tiwa-language-speaking pueblos also create purely artistic forms and animal figures, but the range of pottery differs. Picuris remains beautifully traditional, while Taos seeks a diversity equal to the tourists who visit there.

Micaceous clay fires to a beautiful gold or tan, and the specular highlights which glitter from a pot's surface are due to the many tiny flakes of mica that occur naturally in this clay. Micaceous

Within any given pottery tradition, change can range from subtle to dynamic. This pitcher shape is relatively new, while the appliquéd band and bumps are traditional to Picuris pottery. Not only do they add to the pitcher's beauty, but they enable the vessel to be picked up and handled more easily. Anthony Durand

All micaceous potters claim, with evident enthusiasm, that you haven't tasted good beans until you've cooked some in a seasoned micaceous pot. (Ask your potter for their favorite family recipe!) Micaceous pots are a marriage of art and function. The Taos bean pot on the left (by Virginia T. Romero) and the Picuris serving bowl on the right (by Virginia Duran) were intended for daily use. Kept and used for many years, micaceous pots develop a beautiful patina, the gradual mellowing of surface color due to aging.

When the fire has died and the pot cooled, before the pottery can be seen and removed, there is a time common to all potters that is full of anticipation. Did it crack? Is the color right? There may be no finer time for a potter than that first glimpse of a pot after a successful firing. Anthony Durand proudly shows a newly fired pot.

Children are an important element in pottery making. They help collect materials and provide inspiration, and are often potters themselves. At Picuris Pueblo, Celestino (left) and Wayne Yazza know pottery as more than something to do when the television is off. Their pottery activity contributes to the overall economic well-being of the family.

It is the role of elder potters and those who respectfully follow the tradition to guide the younger generations along each step of the pottery-making process. For Frances Martinez of Picuris Pueblo, this means teaching the young to offer prayers and offerings to the "Clay Lady" before gathering clay. "By doing this," she says, "the clay will always be there for you."

clay is generally found in mountainous areas and, like all natural clays, is produced by the chemical decomposition of igneous and metamorphic rocks. Its primary component is hydrous aluminum silicate particles. Impure organic matter gathered into the clay during the sedimentary process provides its earthy aroma. Clay varies by location, leading to great and subtle variations in its working plasticity, strength, and final color. Picuris pottery tends to be thinner, harder, and lighter in color due to such fine differences.

Before the Pueblo Revolt of 1680, both pueblos produced black-on-whiteware. It is possible that contact with their Apache neighbors to the west during the time of the revolt resulted in the change to micaceous clay. Micaceous pottery is undergoing a revival with many new artists emerging into this wonderful tradition.

San Juan

Like many other pueblos, San Juan is built, in part, on the hallowed grounds of historic and pre-historic Pueblo sites. Walking through fertile fields or along a dirt road, it is possible to find potsherds dating back to A.D. 1475. The San Juan pottery tradition of today is actually the result of potters taking that walk in the 1930s, finding shards and deciding to re-create this old tradition. This "new-old" style features a polished red rim and base with an unslipped, buff-colored band around the middle. The band is incised, and micaceous slip is applied to the incised lines before firing.

Contemporary variations on this approach include decorating the middle band with red, buff, and white matte paints, incising, or carving polychrome vessels. Designs are generally geometric, floral, or borrowed from ancient shards.

San Juan clay is hard, entangled with tree roots, and difficult to gather. As a result, many San Juan potters get their clay from other sources.

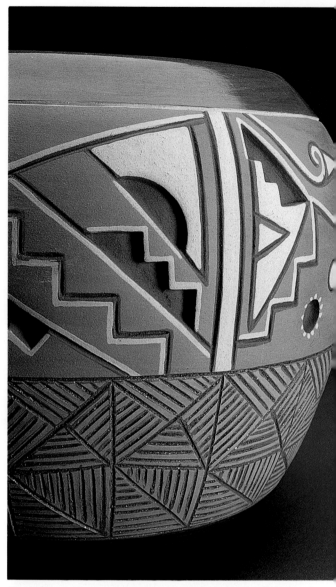

Two decorative techniques are shown here. Carving (top half) is the act of removing rather large amounts of clay from a pot's surface with X-acto® knives and other tools before it dries too hard. Incising (bottom half) is the cutting of closely spaced lines into the surface of the pot while it is hard, but before firing. This technique creates dynamic visual patterns. Whereas carved surfaces can be slipped, polished, and painted, incised surfaces are generally left alone, allowing the natural clay color and texture to show their own beauty. Rosita and Norman DeHerrera

During historic time gourd pieces, dried corn, sticks, and stones were the primary tools used for decorating pottery. Today, like many potters elsewhere, those at San Juan Pueblo explore the modern world with renewed creative energy looking for decorative tools. Tongue depressors, pieces of plastic, metal, and other items have found their way into the potter's tool arsenal. This inventive pattern was made by pressing a right-angled piece of wood or metal into the curved clay surface while it was relatively soft. Diego Aguino

The pueblo of San Juan, referred to by its members as Ohkay Owingeh, "place of the strong people," lies near the confluence of the Chama River and the Rio Grande about 35 miles north of Santa Fe, New Mexico.

San Juan is home to the Eight Northern Indian Pueblo Arts and Crafts Fair held in July. Hundreds of artists, including dozens of potters, sell their work. Another good place to see a variety of San Juan pottery is at the Oke Oweenge Co-op Gallery located in the middle of the pueblo. The co-op shows other forms of pueblo art and conducts classes in the traditional arts for pueblo members.

While differences in the basic pottery style between communities may blur, individual families and artists generally develop recognizable trademarks. The few potters at San Juan are easily recognized by their individual look. Where Diego Aguino prefers a more abstract and textured surface, Alvin Curran opts for a smoother, painted surface. His two pots are decorated with Pueblo cloud, lightning, feather, and sun-faced katsina motifs.

For a carved pot to be successful, it must first be constructed thicker than usual so that the cut areas will have strength. This creates a greater opportunity for cracking or exploding in the firing as there is more chance of the clay containing imperfections and air pockets. The clay for these fine finished pieces went through an arduous process of cleaning, straining, and curing to ensure its quality. Dominguita Naranjo, Rosita and Norman DeHerrera

Nambe, Pojoaque, and Tesuque

The pottery of these three small neighbor pueblos 5 to 15 miles north of Santa Fe is diverse but shares a similar history.

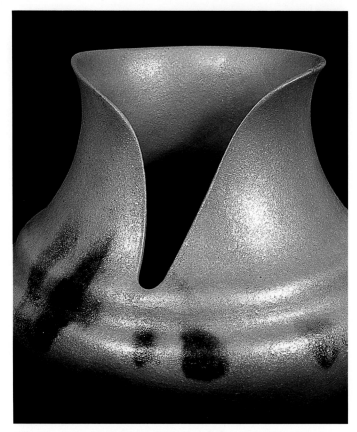

Fire clouds are created when fuel falls against a vessel during firing. The dark surface smudge can add a touch of unexpected beauty to a pot. Lonnie Vigil

NAMBE

Along with its dance and ceremonial culture, the pottery tradition in Nambe has struggled to survive. In reclaiming its heritage, Nambe received help from neighboring Tewa pueblos. As a result, the pottery styles of Nambe bear resemblance to those of other pueblos—polychromes with a polished background and textured matte surface, polished red- and blackware, figurines, and micaceous ware.

One Nambe potter has raised the making of micaceous pottery to the level of fine art. As a young man, Lonnie Vigil was working for the Bureau of Indian Affairs in Washington, D.C. Wanting a change he returned home and "discovered pottery." His refinement of technique and successful attempts at building large vessels has brought world recognition to this small pueblo.

Vigil represents an emerging trend in pottery making—man as a primary pottery maker. In the beginning, although men helped collect clay, build, design, and fire the pottery, it was usually the women who assumed the leadership role. In the past few decades more men have turned to pottery to provide for their families, satisfy their need to create, and earn a living without having to leave the pueblo. Nurtured by the aunts and grandmothers in their families, men such as Lonnie Vigil make pottery as beautiful and bold, as delightful and delicate, as their female peers.

POJOAQUE

Like its neighbor Nambe, the pottery tradition at Pojoaque Pueblo is sparse and mainly derived from other pueblos. However, the few active potters create a profusion of quality pieces. Traditional micaceous bean pots and utility ware share the sales shelf with a diverse array of modern micaceous shapes inspired by Pueblo philosophy.

Potters also create polychrome pottery, painting multi-colored, pale-hued, geometric designs on off-white, tan, or polished red vessels.

The pueblo itself was resettled and revived in the 1930s after being abandoned about 20 years earlier. Pottery is holding its own despite the lure of pueblo-owned casino and service industry jobs.

In response to increased interest in traditional culture, the pueblo of Pojoaque has built a fine new museum and cultural center. Called the Poeh Center, its architecture is modeled after Anasazi structures at Chaco and Mesa Verde. There, area Pueblo artists teach a variety of traditional and contemporary arts to Pueblo people in northern New Mexico. It is through these classes that the pottery tradition at Pojoaque will continue to prosper.

Bea Tioux, an artist and educator versatile in clay, drums, and embroidery, believed strongly in reviving the art of Tesuque Pueblo, and so opened her own gallery to offer her people and the public a consistent source of artwork. She features micaceous ware made by her and her extended family.

TESUQUE

Being close to Santa Fe, the pottery tradition of Tesuque Pueblo has both benefited and suffered. Fine painted pottery was abandoned in the wake of tourism beginning in the 1880s. In response to the demand for souvenirs, Tesuque produced great quantities of polychrome pottery, brightly poster-painted figurines including the Tesuque "rain god."

Today's Tesuque potters are looking for a tradition and are finding it in micaceous ware. Canteens, bowls, vases, and plates are becoming common. Some have designs painted in black, but most are plain. Painted figures of deer and other animals are also emerging. And the collectors are returning.

In response to the increasing pottery market, pueblo members are once again making high quality pottery. Like a growing number of potters throughout the Southwest, several have opened their own galleries in the pueblo. Native-owned galleries allow artists to overcome the high financial overhead or low profit margin associated with opening a city gallery or selling to one. They also create economic and artistic interest within their community. The old tradition is being reborn here.

The persistent "Tesuque Rain God" was first commissioned by a candy manufacturer as a sales promotion. It had nothing to do with religious beliefs but caught on and is even being "revived" today. Historic, unsigned

At Pojoaque the mother/son (back/front) team of Cordi and Glen Gomez creates a wide variety of nature-inspired traditional and contemporary micaceous pottery. Cordi's was among the first families to resettle the pueblo and is credited with reinvigorating the pottery tradition.

Cochiti

Contemporary Cochiti pottery is almost entirely devoted to the making of storytellers and figurines. But this was not always the case. Historic collections show that Cochiti potters made a variety of utilitarian bowls, pitchers, and plates. These were painted black on cream vessels with red occasionally added to the design.

The building of Cochiti Dam destroyed the gray clay source, and made the white slip difficult to find. Cochiti potters used to buy or trade for it from Santo Domingo potters, but its scarcity has led to price increases. As a result, Cochiti potters are now searching for their own cache of slip. This often requires digging 6 to 12 feet into the ground.

Historic Cochiti potters also made fanciful figurines in the shape of animals, birds, and humans, reminiscent of prehistoric effigy pots. Among them was the "Singing Mother," a single, open-mouthed, madonna-like figure with child.

Helen Cordero is credited with creating the new tradition of storytellers. As a young girl she

The story is told that Clay Old Woman and Clay Old Man went into the village where she began making clay while he danced and sang. While dancing, Clay Old Man broke a pot. Clay Old Woman got angry and chased him. They soon made up. Clay Old Man gave the broken clay to everyone in the village. And that is how the people of Cochiti learned pottery. "Snowflake Flower" Stephanie Rhoades

used to listen to her grandfather tell stories to children in the pueblo who climbed all over him and sat on his lap to listen. As a potter in the 1960s, Cordero recalled those times with fondness. When folk art collector Alexander Girard encouraged her to expand on the singing mother idea by adding multiple children, she fashioned her first storyteller figures. They were an immediate artistic and economic success. Since then dozens of potters have borrowed, adapted, and extended the storyteller idea to their own creative cultural liking.

Helen Cordero's storyteller figures always have the mouth open and the eyes closed to "better see the story." Her first was made in 1964 and had five children. It was inspired by her grandfather, Santiago Quintana, who told stories to maintain cultural traditions.

Today you can find storytellers as turtles, bears, frogs, coyotes, owls, other animals, and a variety of people. Figurines, called *monos*, are making a dynamic comeback, often poking fun at tourist and museum stereotypes. This form of energy adds to the overall creativity of all potters. The phenomenon of the Cochiti storyteller tradition is that the figures that once created the market are now determined by the market they created!

Today you can find a vast variety of people and animals as storytellers. Instead of just hanging onto the teller in realistic fashion, the listening children can be seen climbing, falling, and racing across the larger figure. There seems no end to the creative playfulness that making a storyteller figure inspires. There also seems to be an unstated competition among potters to see who can place the most children on a single storyteller—the current record is over 100! (Left to right) Seferina Ortiz, Felicita Eustace, Snowflake Flower (2), Mary O. Chalam

Human-like figurines, called monos, are being reinvented today. They show up in historic photographs as early as 1880. By contrast, glossy advertisements for fine art galleries show Virgil Ortiz's monos dressed in black leather and chains, presenting themselves as the bad boys of Pueblo pottery. Bowls and animal effigy pots are also being made with renewed vigor. Ivan Lewis, Virgil Ortiz, Helen Cordero

Santo Domingo and San Felipe

SANTO DOMINGO

Santo Domingo pottery is characterized by large and gracefully balanced floral, bird, and leaf designs most often painted in black and red on a cream-slip base. The primary forms are dough bowls, stew bowls, and a variety of water jars and canteens.

Today's Santo Domingo pottery is made mostly in two traditional styles. Kiua polychrome

The making of traditional pottery is led by Robert Tenorio of Santo Domingo Pueblo, whose fine painted vessels are often decorated with ancient Mimbres-like designs, such as the bighorn and turkey on this double canteen.

has graceful, black, geometric patterns divided into vertical panels painted on the cream-colored slip body. The underbody is usually painted in a solid red slip. Older pots in this style (pre-1930) often had a polished red stripe over the top of the matte-red bottom. Red appears in the upper-body designs.

"Reverse-painting" is a technique begun about 1910 by the Aguilar family at the prompting of a local merchant. The basic Kiua cream-colored slip base is almost all covered with red and black painted designs. The insides of dough bowls and other vessels are often painted entirely red.

Historic black- and redwares (no longer made) bear the flower, leaf, and animal designs typical of the other styles.

The paint of choice for all Santo Domingo

Santo Domingo pottery, like that of Hopi, Acoma, Zia, and others, is categorized as having a dull matte or semi-matte finish. This refers to the lack of high-gloss stone polishing seen on northern Pueblo pottery. The matte finish allows the vegetal and mineral clay paints to exhibit their natural beauty. Paulita Pacheco

pottery types is boiled down Rocky Mountain bee plant, a tall purple-flowered plant that grows in great abundance across the Southwest. To create the paint, large bunches of the plant are collected. The flower and stalk are put in a large pot and boiled down. This is done outside as the process is odorous. Once boiled down, the concentrated sludge is scooped out and allowed to dry. It serves much like a cake of watercolor. Using yucca-leaf brushes, the potter paints a design. The paint goes on ocher in color but fires to a dark gray to rich black depending on the concentration of the paint. Cream, white, and red colors are watered-down clay. These slips are then painted on the pottery with a brush.

Santo Domingo pottery lives in the shadow of its well-known jewelry industry. As the market and supply costs change, the talented people of Santo Domingo sometimes alternate between jewelry and pottery. As a result of the persistence of a few, many Santo Domingo families now make a good living by carrying on a valued tradition.

SAN FELIPE

The pottery tradition of San Felipe is deeply hidden within this conservative pueblo. Historic forms of pottery made at San Felipe are a rough brownware and a polychrome, and indicate heavy borrowing from styles based in Santa Clara, Santo Domingo, Laguna, and Jemez. As is sometimes the case in other pueblos, the "best" potters to be found in San Felipe during the 1970s and 80s were not natives, but married into the pueblo from neighboring Jemez.

The content and design of all Southwest pottery is either inspired or limited by each

Inspiration has many sources, from natural to man-made. Inventive potters like Hubert Candelario of San Felipe explore them all. The bottom and top pieces are from the melon bowl tradition. Check the sole of your sandals for a possible explanation for the other.

community's traditional beliefs. Figurative pottery made for sale is specifically denied at San Felipe. This is also true of several other pueblos in the area—Zia, Santa Ana, and Santo Domingo.

It is often said that creativity cannot exist in a vacuum. There is one potter at San Felipe who has defied that adage. Hubert Candelario creates unique micaceous forms that increasingly are more abstract and sculptural than functional. Seemingly inspired by the great Pueblo pottery tradition surrounding him in New Mexico, Candelario may be establishing a tradition where there hasn't been much of one in decades.

When Andrew Pacheco of Santo Domingo Pueblo was young, he took his normal first-grader's fascination with dinosaurs and put it to clay. Refined and matured, both artist and dinosaur still work together, with profits going to Andrew's growing computer center.

27

Jemez

Whereas most pottery traditions take hundreds of years to develop, the current tradition at Jemez developed during only a few decades. The Jemez "look" includes polishing pink clay to a brownish-red complemented by large areas left matte. Potters at Jemez use a wide variety of forms and techniques. Appliqué, incising, sculpture, and warm-tone, multi-colored slips can be found on large jars, seed jars, wedding vases, canteens, storytellers, and a wide variety of figurines including owls and clowns.

Pottery traditions are subject to a variety of economic, cultural, and tourist-oriented obstacles that either encourage them to prosper or lead them to disappear, only to revive once conditions become favorable. The pottery tradition

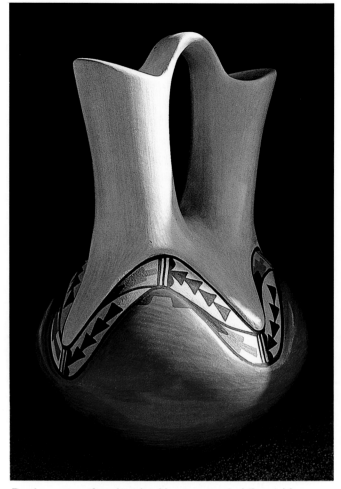

Designs are often inspired by personal philosophies. Marie Romero describes her wedding vase— "where the sky and snow mingle with the ground, there flows the river of health and happiness."

at Jemez has run the gauntlet, moving from tradition to tourist kitsch, back to tradition, and now, on to innovation.

The historic tradition dates back to A.D. 1200, when potters in the Jemez Mountains made black-on-whiteware similar to Mesa Verde black-on-white. During their migration to the current pueblo between the Jemez and Salado rivers, these Towa-speaking people lost their tradition and became farmers, buying the clay vessels they needed from potters at Zuni with crops. In 1598, Spanish Governor Oñate declared them converted to Catholicism. Jemez lay in cultural dormancy until modern times when cultural dances and ceremonies were re-introduced.

Pottery making began its revival during the

Recent pottery from Jemez shows a strong orientation to fine-art quality. Etched, painted, and carved pottery rivals the pottery in communities with a stronger tradition. Jemez pottery has come full circle, and now stands on its own. (Clockwise from upper right) Ponca Fragua, Geraldine Sandi S. Chinana, Carol F. Gachupin, Carol Vigil

Responding to the artistic and economic success of storytellers made in Cochiti Pueblo, potters at Jemez quickly and uniquely adapted the concept to their own styles. Today Jemez rivals Cochiti as a source for original, playful, and well-made figures. Storytellers delight both creators and collectors. Chris and Vera Fragua, Cheryl Fragua, Laura Fragua, J. Pecos

Great Depression when potters copied the un-fired, poster-paint pieces made at Tesuque. This style continued through the 1960s, when the hippie phenomenon popularized anything Indian. In the early 1970s, several insightful potters saw that quality, hand-built pottery was bringing good prices. Their success prompted a tremendous growth in the quality, quantity, and diversity of pottery forms made throughout the 1980s and 90s. That creative explosion sustains Jemez pottery to this day.

Native artists often encourage quality in each other by purchasing or trading for each other's work. Fine art sculptor Cliff Fragua encouraged his aunts' and other potters' best work by buying them. Jemez pottery is alive today because the people have persisted in maintaining an individual and cultural identity in the face of adversity.

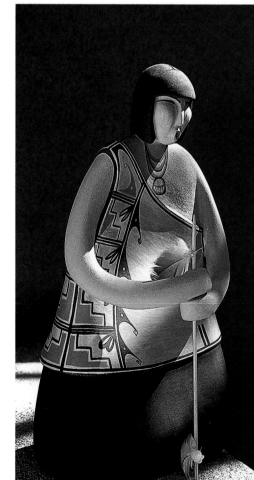

Corn is a staple of the traditional Indian diet and one of the primary clans in many Southwest cultures. "Corn Maiden" by Maxine Toya honors her connection to this sacred food.

A Life in Clay -
A Conversation with Marie Romero

Like most potters Marie Romero, from the pueblo of Jemez, shares a special relationship with the clay. She knows that working in clay is much more than a job.

"Clay is everything to me. It's a spirit that is just as alive as I am. Everything I have—my home, my kids, their education, many of my friends—whatever I have at home is all from clay. Because of this we treat it differently. We treat it with great respect. I talk to the clay, you know, praying, because it's how I make my living and it's a part of me. Before I start working with the clay, I take a little piece of it and pray for the spirits of all the great potters who have passed on, various people who have inspired me, and deceased relatives. I ask them for their guidance.

"And it's true, the clay does speak to you, because it's a living thing. It knows what shape it wants to be when you are forming it. It takes in your thoughts and feelings. If your heart and mind are in the right place when you are building, designing, and firing, then it will come out beautiful. It makes you feel good to make a beautiful pot—and when someone falls in love with your pot and buys it, it just makes you feel so much better knowing that something you made could make someone feel like that."

Marie Romero making a small wedding vase. Marie belongs to the Corn Clan, so she often paints or appliqués an image of corn on her pottery.

While raising children and developing her pottery, Marie taught kindergarten at the Jemez Pueblo Day School. She says that story time was the children's favorite. Taking her inspiration from a children's nursery rhyme, Marie Romero created "There Was an Old Woman Who Lived in a Shoe," taking cultural and artistic license to humorously change the shoe to an Indian moccasin.

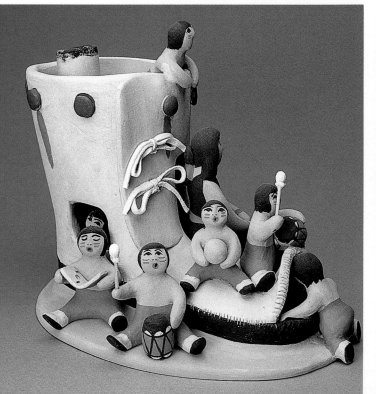

The Art and Work of Pottery Making

Ask any potter and they will tell you that work and play are the same when it comes to making pottery. While many books, exhibits, galleries, and collectors place importance on the object, it is of greater importance and insight to remember that the making of pottery is a human event. The process from collecting to selling can take months, with each step requiring care and the help of family. The sequence of events is laden with personal, family, and cultural meaning.

Contemporary American Indian potters come from cultures whose traditions teach that they, as individuals and as a people, are one with the earth. The making of handmade clay pottery is a direct expression of that belief. Clay is viewed as a living entity, a gift from what Pueblo potters respectfully call the "Clay Mother."

Natural earth clays are found throughout the Southwest. Potters usually use the family source, and gathering clay is a family event. The potter, spouse, children, and often parents participate in the task. An uncle's truck may be borrowed. A sibling has baked fresh bread for the midday meal. At the clay pit a prayer is offered. The potter then takes only the clay he or she needs.

Clay is first soaked and screened to remove unwanted debris. It then undergoes highly individualized cleaning processes which involve soaking, screening, drying, and repeated screening through smaller screens. Most clays require a temper, the addition of sand or volcanic ash, to prevent cracks during drying and firing. The preparation of clay is labor intensive, and the attention to detail at this stage is the basis for quality work. Once prepared, the clay is placed in containers where it remains until the potter is ready to build.

preparing wet clay
Randy Nahohai, Zuni

While shaping clay, potters commonly speak about "talking with the clay," meaning the clay also has a voice in determining its final shape. Two building methods are generally used—pinching for miniatures and some figures, and the more common rope-like coil method for larger pots and sculptural figures. A pot is begun with a thin slab of clay usually pressed into a "puki" or starter bowl. The potter builds by applying a series of hand-rolled coils to the base. Each coil is pressed into the previous one, smoothed, and scraped. Throughout building, potters feel for tiny air pockets and impurities that could crack a pot in firing. The process is continued until the rough form is finished.

building a pot with coils
Tina Garcia, Santa Clara

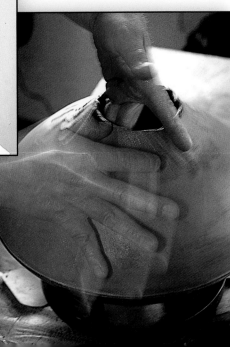

forming the opening
Glen Gomez, Pojoaque

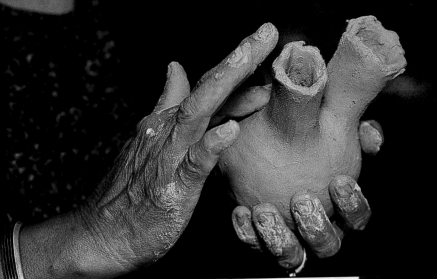

To finish a pot, it is first smoothed with small amounts of water applied by hand or sponge. At this point the various styles of pottery diverge in the process. Micaceous, red- and blackware, or pieces to be painted are set aside to dry. Pots that receive carving or appliqué continue to be worked on. Tools include fingers, tongue depressors, and X-acto® knives. The pots are then dried and sanded.

smoothing the final form
Marie Romero, Jemez

carving a design
Marie Romero, Jemez

The process of "decorating" a pot begins with creating a smooth surface. The sanded surface is painted with a clay slip and then polished with smooth stones or left matte (unpolished). A high gloss is achieved by making repeated passes with the stone over a single area.

polishing
with stone
Tina Garcia,
Santa Clara

Natural paint comes in three forms—clay, vegetal, and mineral—offering a variety of colors. Some potters paint with modern brushes, but those who make the fine-lined designs found on Acoma and Hopi pots prefer brushes made from yucca plants. Traditional paints are applied before the firing, thereby making them an integral part of the finished pot.

painting unfired surface
Elvis Torres, San Ildefonso

Many potters believe that firing makes the pottery a "finished being." Traditional pottery is fired outdoors in wood or manure kilns which reach 1,300 degrees Fahrenheit. Pots are covered by pieces of metal or shards. Fuel is carefully stacked and lit. Time and temperature are measured by experience. Once cooled, the pottery is cloth polished and readied for sale.

firing outdoors
Jean Sahme, Hopi

decorating using sgraffito
Debra Trujillo-Duwyenie, Santa Clara

cooling after firing
Anthony Durand, Picuris

Many pottery styles are finished once they have been fired. Most sgraffito artists wait until after firing to decorate their pieces as they prefer to etch a hard surface. Navajo pottery achieves its look after firing when the warm pots are brushed with heated piñon pitch. Acrylic paints are always applied after firing.

Pottery was historically sold to traders and wholesalers. In modern times many potters work with galleries, have shops of their own, or sell their work at tribal cooperatives. In keeping with tradition, pottery can still be purchased daily on the Portal in Santa Fe as it has been for over a century.

selling at Indian-owned shop
Elvis Torres and Adelphia Martinez,
San Ildefonso

33

Santa Ana, Sandia, Zia, and Isleta

SANTA ANA AND SANDIA

Santa Ana is an agricultural community which has traditionally purchased needed pottery from their Zia neighbors. As a result, there is little pottery currently made at Santa Ana, which struggles to maintain a tradition. The last great Santa Ana pottery matriarch died in the early 1990s. Most tribal members farm or work at the tribally-owned Prairie Star Casino.

Sandia is a tiny pueblo that is being overwhelmed by Albuquerque's urban sprawl. Its economy relies upon one casino and the Bien Mur craft store. Most current pottery is being made by potters from neighboring pueblos who have married into Sandia.

The world awaits the development of a unique style at both Santa Ana and Sandia.

Canteens were an important part of Pueblo life. Farmers may have used such vessels while toiling in the fields. This unsigned Zia piece dates from the early 1900s.

ZIA

By contrast, Zia Pueblo has a strong and stable pottery tradition. Potters at Zia make highly stylized polychrome pottery, a black and red design on a cream- or sand-colored slip with a red base. Zia pottery usually has high shoulders. Distinctive roadrunner-like, split-tailed bird and floral designs are the most common designs on these thick-walled, well-made pots.

Some potters attempt to emulate traditional pottery by giving their new work an old look by scarring, staining, or otherwise aging the surface. This is usually not done to fool the buyer, but to meet artistic needs. The two front Santa Ana pots were painted to make them seem old. (Top to bottom) John Montoya, Frank and Virginia Ortiz (2)

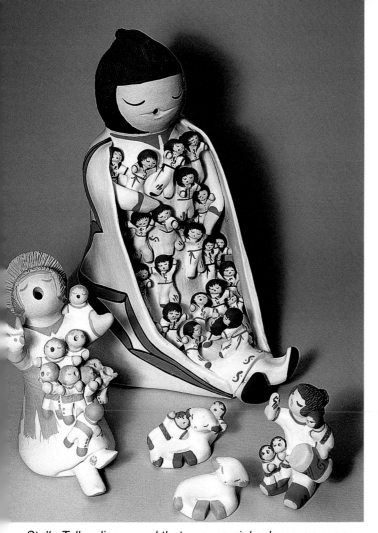

Isleta

Isleta is a large pueblo located on the Rio Grande south of Albuquerque. First settled about A.D. 1200, Isleta has suffered cultural erosion. The first Catholic mission was built in 1613, and the pueblo has been influenced by Hispanic populations ever since. The oldest Isleta pottery was a plain red-brownware bowl used for baking. Potters moving into Isleta from Laguna introduced their polychrome style, and tourist items were made until the Great Depression when the pottery tradition disappeared.

Isleta's current pottery tradition is the direct result of one person's work. In the late 1970s Stella Teller gave up hairdressing and became a full-time potter, launching a whole new tradition at Isleta. She adapted the storyteller idea from Helen Cordero, painting her figures in pastel blue-grays and light tans. They became an immediate success, and today the Teller family dominates pottery production at Isleta. Other families in the pueblo work primarily in polychrome pottery or glass.

Stella Teller discovered that commercial colors won over customers unconcerned with natural pigments or cultural tradition. As a result, many family members and other Isleta people make a good living selling their delightful pastel pottery. Mona and Nicol Teller

Many Indian artists are multi-talented and easily excel in more than one art form. Painters Marcellus Medina (white pots) and Ralph Aragon are equally at home on paper, canvas, or clay. Unlike their natural clay counterparts, these acrylic paints can only be applied on fired pottery. The work of these painters successfully blends techniques of fine art and pottery.

Being water-poor but pottery-rich, Zia residents have traded pottery for food with their neighbor pueblos for over 200 years. Of the same Keresan language as Acoma and Laguna, Zia potters share the same aesthetic zest for geometric patterns, rainbows, flowers, and stylized birds. The traditional Zia sun symbol, sometimes used on pots, has become synonymous with New Mexico. It appears on the state flag and license plates. Another painted feature is the "rainbow band," a single or double outlined band that arcs across one side of the vessel.

In a rare departure from tradition, several Zia potters are addressing the need to create personally expressive pottery. Using acrylic paints on otherwise traditional pots, members of the Medina family paint realistic figures on their pottery. Ralph Aragon initiated painting traditional elements in "painterly" arrangements with acrylic on hand-built clay pots. Acrylic work certainly has a place in the pantheon of Pueblo pottery.

Acoma and Laguna

ACOMA

Acoma is world famous for its thin-walled white pottery. Intricate, eye-dazzling, geometric designs, and a range of other figures (including parrots, rainbows, lizards, ladybugs, and Mimbres people and animal figures) adorn pots which range in size from large ollas to tiny miniatures. A vegetal black, red clay, and commercial colors are employed in painting.

Acoma clay is plain white, and clay sources, understandably, remain a secret. It is hard and durable, but (due to gypsum crystals in the clay) subject to spalling—where a small piece breaks off of the surface during firing or long afterwards.

According to legend, Acoma's hero twins led the ancestors to Ako, the magic white rock that would be their home. This large, 1,500-foot-high mesa in west-central New Mexico is commonly known as Sky City. Although most of the community lives on the lands below, it is the village in the sky that is most recognized. The village is kept traditional—no electricity, no amenities. Soil is hauled up from the valley; water is caught in cisterns.

The animal kingdom is often celebrated on Southwest pottery for all Indian cultures have a strong expressed relationship to animals. This Acoma bear is painted with a "heartline" or "breathline," suggesting one way animals and people are connected—we breathe the same air. Mildred Antonio

Potters learn and grow from one another in wonderful ways. These golf-ball-sized story pots are an extension of the classic storyteller. Playful children and their dog roam these pots meant to represent Acoma's carved-rock water cisterns. Corine Garcia

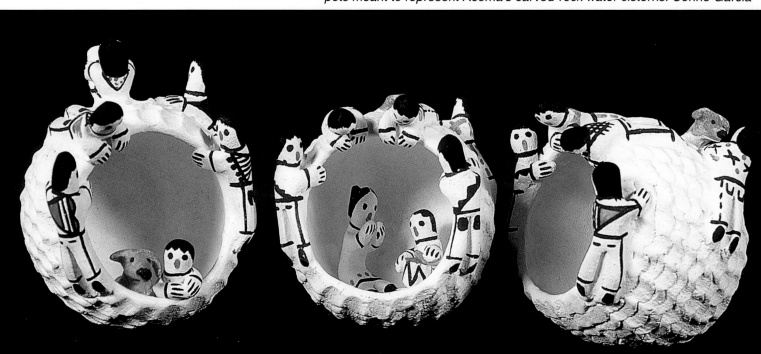

The eye-dazzling, superlative pottery of Acoma artist Dorothy Torivio is a testament to the care and precision that is possible with handmade work. Though the patterns appear computer generated, they are not. Each line and color has been applied with a natural yucca brush.

The twins also led the people to the white clay, the finest in the Southwest. A connection to the past is celebrated in making the temper for pottery. Ancient potsherds are ground and used to help strengthen the vessel. The strength of the old strengthens the new.

Like most pottery traditions, the one at Acoma was begun by family matriarchs. Lucy Lewis and Marie Z. Chino began their careers in the 1920s. As friends they may have shared ideas, one of which was to paint the designs found on ancient potsherds around the pueblo, on new pots. With the encouragement of anthropologist Kenneth Chapman at the Museum of New Mexico, Lucy Lewis furthered her use of ancient forms by studying the museum's collection of Anasazi and Mimbres pottery. Chino and Lewis adapted prehistoric designs, creating optical illusions in black or black and orange paints that miraculously fit the shape of each vessel. These repeated geometric patterns and motifs have become the signature for much of Acoma pottery.

With popularity came the pressure to produce. In the 1960s electric kilns and greenware were introduced at Acoma. A number of Acoma potters have found an economic niche decorating these less expensive molded pots.

Acoma pottery comes in a wide range of form and decoration, all well-crafted. One can find large bowls and pots, figurines, and miniatures decorated with large bold designs or intricate hair-thin abstract line designs. If activity breeds creativity, then Acoma is the queen bee of painted pottery. (Clockwise from bottom left) Nellie V. Garcia, Emma Lewis, Nellie V. Garcia, Marilyn Ray, Sharon and Bernard Lewis

37

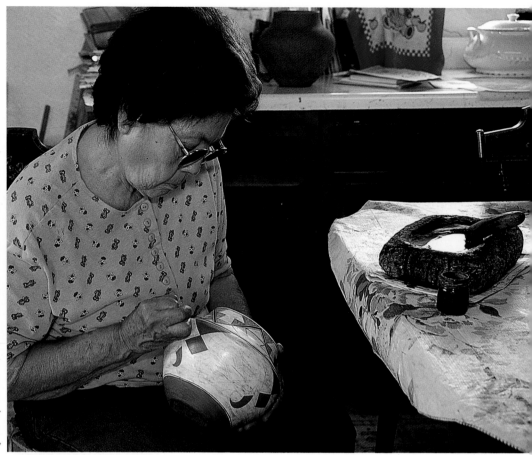

For many potters the kitchen table becomes their "studio" once the breakfast dishes are cleared. Few potters have formal studios, and even those are in the comfort of one's own home. Evelyn Cheromiah, the "dean" of Laguna potters, works daily making pottery in her quiet village home. Here she paints her intricate designs using natural wild spinach paint and a yucca brush. She says of her work, "All that we do comes from how thankful our people were and still are today for the gifts of nature."

Most designs are applied with a yucca brush. A single spear of this hearty desert plant is cut to length and then split to the desired thickness. Paints are primarily vegetal, though a few employ minerals. Plants are gathered and boiled down to make the initial paint paste. Some potters paint directly with this paste, while others dilute it with water or mix it with ground sandstone.

Acoma potters are diverse and productive making pottery as fine as—maybe better than—it has ever been.

LAGUNA

Laguna pottery is often overshadowed by Acoma's, which developed from a similar tradition. Patterns are both geometric and of life-forms, and generally bolder than those of Acoma. Shapes

Acoma potters make a great variety of miniature pottery. Each piece shown here resembles pottery made in larger sizes. Potters practicing the miniature style are challenged to maintain quality in building, a still hand when painting, and good eyesight. Many employ jewelers' glasses or similar devices to magnify the area they are painting. (Clockwise from top left) Lily Salvador, Rainey Naha (Hopi), Rebecca Lucario, Sharon and Bernard Lewis, Sharon Lewis, Sharon and Bernard Lewis, Thomas Natseway (Laguna)

Michael Kanteena's pottery mirrors forms and designs found on pottery created by Anasazi, Mimbres, and other ancient cultures. He carefully studies museum collections and artifacts found in the landscape surrounding his Laguna Pueblo home. He then builds and paints, creating a unique form of pottery that honors the ancestors.

Contrast and similarity within a single style are evident in this Cheromiah family portrait. Many of the designs used are family heirlooms. Created by an elder they were passed down, replicated, and altered through succeeding generations. Beginning when they were children, Evelyn taught her two daughters, LeeAnn and Mary, the finer points of pottery making. Their work is now "as good as mom's," they say, and they are each teaching their children.

include large ollas, bowls, and vases. Some older pieces feature two-coil twisted handles.

The coming of the railroad in 1880, uranium mines in the 1950s, and the constant lure of jobs in Albuquerque almost erased pottery. Motivated by looking at her mother's pottery tools, Evelyn Cheromiah learned to build, and almost single-handedly revived, Laguna pottery by teaching classes through the aid of a federal grant in the 1970s. Only a few of the participants have gone on to make pottery, an example of how difficult it can be for this art form to continue in some communities. A few persisted, and more caught on.

Serving in a "kid sister" role, Laguna's potters have developed widely diverse styles not wholly based on tradition. Laguna now has a growing and thriving pottery tradition worthy of collection.

Melon bowls, like these by Laguna artist Andrew Padilla, were revived from an ancient tradition by Santa Clara potters. Despite their name, they are inspired by squash, a favorite in most Indian fields and at feasts.

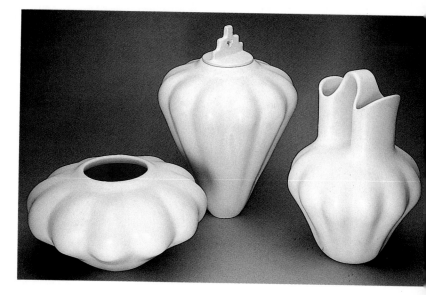

Zuni

Zuni pottery is an active blend of traditional and contemporary work. Potters make ollas, effigy shapes (especially owls), clay baskets, and ceremonial cornmeal bowls.

Unique Zuni designs and motifs include frogs, tadpoles, dragonflies, the Zuni "rain bird," flower rosettes, and deer with painted red "heartlines," as well as other water and hunting symbols. Both older and contemporary Zuni potters like sculpture and appliqué. Clay vessels are often adorned with frogs, lizards, or other important animal symbols, or they may even be shaped as animals.

Some new work is a direct representation of traditional styles, while other artists use tradition as a catalyst for personally expressive, often fanciful designs. Individual potters are setting new standards for creativity.

Zuni is the westernmost New Mexico pueblo and dates back to the 1500s. It is known primarily for its jewelry and fetishes. Pottery made prior to

Each potter has something in mind when creating their design. When purchasing directly from an artist, it can be very rewarding to ask the potter to explain the thought behind the creation. This abstract detail is seen by artist Randy Nahohai as "mating eagles embraced by clouds and rain."

The designs and images painted on Zuni pottery tend to be bolder and often more fanciful than other communities. Most of the pottery shapes are of ancient origin, for Zuni potters have conducted extensive research of their tradition at museums. The humped-back flute player is common, as are "water-beings"—the frogs, toads, and tadpoles who signal the presence of this important resource. (Left to right) Rowena Him, Randy Nahohai, Jack Kalestewa

1930 is rare. It was polychrome, made from Zuni's pinkish clay which was slipped in white or buff and painted with black-brown or red paints. Zuni potters of this period made ollas, baskets, jars, and ceremonial pieces.

By 1950 Zuni's pottery making had given way to a robust economy based on fine, inlaid jewelry. The pottery tradition lay dormant until a series of dedicated artist-teachers began pottery classes at Zuni High School. The first instructors—Daisy Hooee from Hopi, and Jenny Laate of Acoma—were "imported," by marriage, from other pueblos. These classes employed an electric kiln, the preferred method of firing for most Zuni potters today.

Changing silver prices lured a number of jewelers to pottery. In 1985, potter Josephine Nahohai received a fellowship from the School of American

Potters bear a responsibility to their culture as well as to themselves. When clay vessels are required for ceremonial use, select potters are asked to build and donate the pottery necessary. This painted cornmeal bowl with painted polliwogs is a good example. Several plain or specifically painted versions may be requested. The potter abandons all other work, and completes and donates the finished pieces, thereby returning a portion of their creative gift to the tribe. All pieces by Randy Nahohai

Research to study old pottery and teach it to Zuni women. Ironically, her sons became two of Zuni's better potters. In the mid-1980s the Zuni Tribal Arts & Crafts Enterprise, a great supporter of all tribal arts, sent six potters to the Smithsonian to see historic Zuni pottery. The effect on pottery production was immediate. Older shapes and designs appeared and have served as the foundation of a thriving and creative tradition ever since.

Hopi

Hopi is one of the oldest and most widely collected of all the pottery styles. It is descended from pottery made in the area for over a thousand years. It is a clearly defined look marked by reworked ancient Ancestral Puebloan and Sinaguan designs on polished, unslipped, yellow vessels.

The nine villages on the three mesas in north-central Arizona that define Hopi retain a first-world feel. The Third Mesa village of Old Oraibi is said to be the oldest continually inhabited city in the United States, dating back to the twelfth century.

The Hopis' ancestors traded yellowware pottery from the 700s, but with pressure from marauding Spanish, Apache, and Navajo, the trading, and hence the pottery making, declined to almost nothing by the 1800s. After the Pueblo Revolt of 1680, Tewa-speaking fugitives from the northern Rio Grande pueblos hid out at Hopi. They established the village of Hano on First Mesa, the site of most of today's pottery making. In the early 1800s drought and epidemic forced many Hopis to seek refuge among the Zuni. There they relearned pottery.

Nampeyo family members often employ two designs given by Nampeyo—the bird wing or "migration" that encircles this wedding vase, and the "eagle." At any given time, the most celebrated Hopi potters are likely to be Nampeyo descendants. Elva Nampeyo, one of 14 Nampeyo grandchildren

In 1880, trader Thomas Keam, whose trading post still stands today, asked potters to reproduce the pottery designs found in the abandoned village of Sikyatki. When the railroad reached the area in the 1880s, it created a great market for tourist pottery. These events set the stage for the Hopi phenomenon.

The founding story of contemporary Hopi pottery is that of Nampeyo, her relationship with professional ethnologists and archaeologists, and the positive influence they had on her.

Antiquity can be bothersome. Experts and family members say that this fine, unsigned pot may have been made by Nampeyo and possibly painted by her daughter Annie. A Nampeyo signature on a pot of this quality could mean thousands of dollars more for the seller.

In 1896 Smithsonian ethnologist J. Walter Fewkes excavated Sikyatki. He wrote that he'd shown the sixteenth- and seventeenth-century pottery he'd uncovered to the wife of one of his workmen. Familiar with the designs from shards, Nampeyo was impressed by seeing whole pots and adopted both into her work. By 1900, she had become the first celebrity potter in the Southwest. The Fred Harvey Company took her to the Grand Canyon to demonstrate for hotel guests—and to Chicago where she introduced Southwest pottery to the world. Her descendants include approximately 70 potters spread over six generations.

Begun in relative obscurity Nampeyo's style and incredible success have defined Hopi pottery ever since. The Nampeyo connection has brought deserved recognition to all potters at Hopi. Additional families have developed their own styles and have helped make Hopi pottery as diverse and creative as any other.

Hopi potters pride themselves on the "blush" of the pot's surface, the subtle variation of surface color created by fire clouds. Not only beautiful, these marks also serve as proof that a pot was traditionally fired. The distinctive ring you hear when you tap a Hopi pot is a further indication of traditional firing. It means that the clay has been hardened by consistent high temperatures. (From top to bottom) Steve Lucas, Lawrence Namoki, Iris Youvella, Gwen Setalla, Les Namingha (2)

The work of three great contemporary potters demonstrates how inspiration can take many decorative directions. The Dextra Quotskuyva pot in the upper right shows a "classical" amount of surface decoration. Rondina Huma's pot inspired by ancient potsherd designs is quite complex. By contrast, Iris Youvella's pot simply and elegantly states her respect for corn.

The Pottery Tradition -
A Conversation with Jean Sahme

Jean Sahme is a fifth-generation descendant of Nampeyo. The pottery tradition is a constant influence on her life and family.

"Nampeyo gave us a great gift. More than a way to make income, pottery is something she created to be a guide for life. By making pottery you start thinking about the earth, the cornfields, rain, and just life's gifts in general. It helps maintain your family and culture. It teaches you discipline and how to work—because you can't be lazy and make pottery! It really makes you a down-to-earth person. The pottery is not really as important as working on the pottery and having those life, family, and cultural values to practice daily. I humble myself when I think of what she really did.

"I also thank the creator for knowing what we needed and providing it. Everything we use is natural and from the earth. And it's powerful. I mean, once I stuck my hand in the clay, something changed. It kind of erased everything that was outside, the busy, daily activities of the world, you know. When I started pottery I became content.

"Ideas for designs are all around you. When I began, I used my mom's and grandma's. That's how the tradition gets shared. A few of the designs are Nampeyo's. As a family member, I am allowed to use them. Every Hopi pottery design shows elements of nature like corn, clouds, or things that are above. The colors are important, too. Red is the sun or rain. A pot is really personal thoughts, feelings, and ideas about culture made tangible."

Pottery offers more than income and expression. Though pottery was always in her life, Jean Sahme explored careers in education, business, and clerical work before settling on making pottery full time. Her decision was not initiated by the art or family persuasion, but by the birth of her daughter. As a single mother, she felt the need to be home when her daughter came home from school. Pottery has allowed her to do that.

Pottery is a Nampeyo family tradition practiced by all four sisters. Three of the four smaller pots were made by Jean Sahme, and the other by her sister Rachel Sahmie. According to Jean, the designs are traditionally carried through the family by the women. If Jean had a potter son, he could use Nampeyo family designs, but his son could not. The fifth pot was made by Ida Sahme, a Navajo married to Jean's youngest brother. Considered part of the family, she is allowed to employ family clay, but uses imagery from her Navajo heritage.

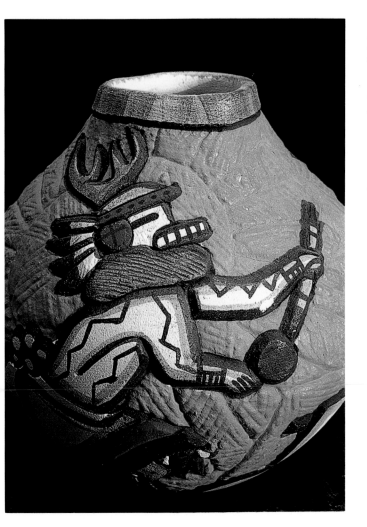

The descendants of Paqua "Frog Woman" Naha have developed her crisply painted whiteware into a recognizable family trademark. Descendants remaining in the family convention make plates, bowls, jars, and vases with intricate black, red, and orange designs. The family of Grace Chapella creates a unique line of pottery, equal in quality to that of the Nampeyo family.

Other Hopi potters are successfully working with boldly carved scenes, incised plainware, Santa Clara-like sgraffito, and finely worked symmetrical and asymmetrical clay sculpture.

Whereas several other pueblos lost their pottery tradition to commercial tourism or gave in to economic pressures and switched to kiln-fired, acrylic-painted greenware, Hopi potters stubbornly persist in maintaining their tradition. Combined with jewelry and katsina carvings, pottery contributes to a healthy family and tribal economy.

A small number of Hopi potters create bold carved pottery that usually depicts portions of ceremonial dance scenes. Begun by Nampeyo descendant Tom Polacca, the style calls for thicker pots, great drawing skill, and an interest in creating textures. To excel at this style, the artist must combine pottery and sculpture skills. Carla Nampeyo, Tom Polacca's daughter

Hopi whiteware is made predominantly by members of another distinguished Hopi pottery family, the Nahas. Paqua Naha signed her work with a drawing of a frog, becoming the first "Frog Woman"—a name continued by her daughter Joy Navasie. Paqua's son married Helen Naha who signed her pottery with a feather, becoming "Feather Woman." Since then, family members on either side have created their own version of the frog or feather signature. Joy Navasie (3 on left), Helen Naha (top right), and daughter Sylvia (bottom right)

Navajo

The most common form of Navajo pottery is the piñon-pitch vessel. The best work is elegant in its simplicity. Most common are double-spouted wedding vases, water jars, bowls, and "bubble" pots, many of which are creative extensions of traditional forms. A wide variety of animal forms are also made. Although much of the pottery is plain, a number of potters excel at appliqué, adding clay forms and designs to the surface of a vessel, and incising patterns into walls.

The coarse clay is dug, cleaned, and shaped by hand. Dried pottery is fired in open, wood and sheep manure fires, resulting in "fire clouds" on the vessels' surface. The final element adding to the uniqueness of Navajo pottery is the application of heated piñon pitch to the just-fired, still hot, pottery. Applied with a pitch-soaked rag, the piñon waterproofs the pot, adding a soft luster and—when it is new—a pungent aroma to the vessel.

Navajos may have learned pottery from Jemez Puebloan people who fled their homeland in the late 1690s, fearing revenge for their part in the Pueblo Revolt of 1680. They sought refuge in the area called Dinetah, the Navajo homeland surrounding present-day Farmington, New Mexico.

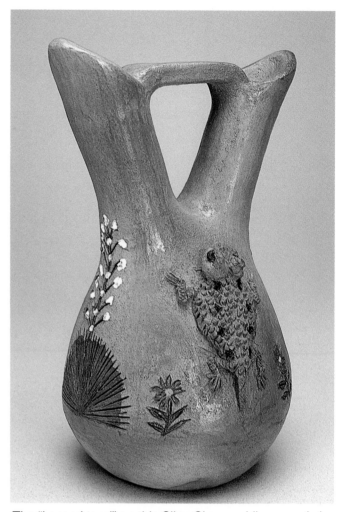

The "horned toad" on this Silas Claw wedding vase is kno to the Navajo as a "grandfather," one of many animals who have respected knowledge. Called a horned lizard by biologists, this creature is believed by Navajos to have power over rain, a valued resource on the dry reservation.

The earliest type of Navajo pottery, Dinetah gray, is characterized by rounded bottoms, thin walls, and rough surface texture created by wiping shredded juniper bark or corncobs over the moist clay. Other historic pottery types include gobernador polychrome, clearly adapted from the Pueblo, Navajo polychrome, and Navajo-piñon gray. Dating back to A.D. 1750-1800, these vessels are smaller and more thickly walled than their predecessors and closely resemble modern forms.

Several factors have led to the slow development of pottery making among the Navajo. Primarily a nomadic people, the Navajo found vessels such as the more pastoral Pueblo used to

The Yei-bi-chei figure etched and painted by Lorraine Williams onto her pot is common in Navajo art. It appears on traditional sandpaintings, silverwork, fine art, rugs, and now pottery. Its roots lie deep in Navajo mythology. To the Navajo, he is Grandfather-of-the-Gods.

The shape and size of historic Navajo pottery was determined by its intended use. Large jars and bowls were required for a variety of utilitarian uses, including cooking and the storage of food and water for long periods of time. These three pots are modern variations on a historic form that would have had a pointed, bullet-shaped bottom enabling the pot to be easily set in the sand. The 30-inch-tall corrugated pot by Louise Goodman reveals its coil construction. A "smooth" version by Rose Williams is next to it. The high-polished front piece by Samuel Manymules is appliquéd with a "ceremonial break." Analogous to the "spirit line" found in many Navajo rugs and baskets, it prevents the maker's creative energies from being trapped in their work.

be too large and breakable for transport. Clays in the Navajo region of the Southwest are generally more coarse, so pottery making is difficult. The rapid rise of weaving and silversmithing eclipsed pottery in economic importance. The introduction of trading posts curtailed the functional use of pottery as Navajos traded their rugs and jewelry for glass, metal, and crockery containers. The easy availability of Anglo goods created disinterest in learning pottery among the younger generations.

With domestic use falling, the most extensive use of Navajo pottery was in Navajo ceremonialism. However, Navajo medicine men strictly dictated its forms and the potter's behavior. In fear of causing spiritual harm to themselves or their families by accidentally breaking the restrictions, most Navajos simply stopped making pottery.

The persistence of Navajo pottery in modern times is directly related to the special attention given to it over a period of more than 40 years by one non-Indian trader. In the early 1940s, William "Bill" Beaver began working at Chaco Canyon, where Navajo pottery sparked his interest. By 1950 he had found work at the Shonto Trading Post in northern Arizona. There he encouraged pottery making and sold a few crates of pitch pots to Tucson trader Tom Bahti, whose son Mark continues the family business. The market was born.

According to Navajo belief, pottery making was one of the gifts given to them by the Holy People before the Navajo emerged into the present world. Pottery's significance is preserved in oral history, ceremonial texts, and songs. Ida Sahmie, a Navajo potter married into the prestigious Nampeyo family of Hopi, uses Hopi pottery to make distinctive clay forms honoring her culture's pottery tradition. The Yei-bi-chei figure is surrounded by painted Navajo wedding baskets. The stepped pattern on the baskets and circling the top of the pot represent sacred Navajo mountains.

The Navajo are primarily known for their handwoven rugs and silver jewelry. Lorraine Williams has borrowed elements from a "storm pattern" design found in both and etched it into her 30-inch-tall jar. Large jars were once quite common as they served to store food and water. Few potters make such pieces today as it takes great skill and patience, and they are not easily sold.

Beaver continued to purchase pottery for his Sacred Mountain Trading Post and his growing personal collection. Soon he was wholesaling throughout the area. Positive changes in the Navajo economy, relaxed religious restrictions on pottery, and increased consumer interest in Navajo pottery merged beginning in the early 1970s, creating an environment for the art to grow. Museums began augmenting their collections by adding Navajo pottery, and Navajo potters began receiving recognition in area shows. Individual variations and innovations in vessel forms and design elements, plus a concentrated improvement of overall quality, took hold.

Pottery is practiced today by a growing number of Navajos, both male and female. Most

More Navajo artisans are turning to clay sculpture as a means of expressing themselves. Natural and commercial clay figurines like these by Elizabeth Abeyta, and masks dominate that scene.

Navajo pottery is moving in three directions—classic piñon-pitch brownware, fine art, and folk art. Folk art pieces are characterized by the use of appliqué, animal forms, and a touch of Navajo whimsy. Silas Claw's bowl decorated with cows in a corral is a good example of this genre which includes piggy banks and mud toys. Alice Cling's glossy, wax-paper-polished jars began the movement into fine art. The wedding vase by Elizabeth Manygoats is an anchor of the classic style.

potters reside in the Shonto-Cow Springs area and tend to be related by marriage or family.

With a renewed tradition creating small but helpful economies, more and more families are making pottery. Those potters who led the Navajo pottery revival have given their people and descendants a wonderful gift. Though pottery as an art form will remain secondary among the Navajo to weaving and silversmithing, it has brought a renewed sense of cultural pride and another means of expressing oneself.

Tohono O'odham

The Tohono O'odham, once known as the Papago, live about a hundred miles southwest of Tucson, Arizona, in the heart of the Sonoran Desert. They live in a dozen small villages, with Sells serving as the tribal center.

Once known primarily for coiled baskets made of bear grass, devil's claw, and yucca, the Tohono O'odham are reviving a pottery tradition that is sure to stand the test of time. Occupying the same lands as the ancient Hohokam (from whom they claim descent), the O'odham have

Modern Tohono O'odham pottery gains inspiration from all elements of their culture. The figure and etched lines on the pot are derived from the man-in-the-maze design common to O'odham basketry, while the form and coarse clay choice are reminiscent of ancient pottery. Billy Manuel

Friendship bowls have been the staple of Tohono O'odham pottery for years. First created by potters from the tiny town of Hickiwan in the mid-1970s, they represent a traditional social round dance. Due to their great appeal, they have become the "storyteller" phenomenon of O'odham pottery. Angea and Manuel families

The Native people who live in the Sonoran Desert of southern Arizona today are the descendants of ancient Hohokam and Salado people who lived within this landscape since the beginning of the desert some 12,000 years ago. Tohono O'odham potters are exploring their cultural history for designs and insight. Like most other pottery communities, the O'odham collect natural clay and paint materials from the earth. Most O'odham pottery is decorated with painted designs of mesquite sap and fired using mesquite as fuel. Manuel family

been making pottery for a long time. The dating of O'odham pottery makes it difficult to say when the first pieces were made. It is also possible that O'odham pottery has been confused with Pima or Gila River pottery. Prior to 1880, these early pieces were very large, undecorated, bulbous storage and water jars made from natural clays that fired to a brownish-red or tan color.

After 1880, O'odham potters switched to black-on-red Maricopa-like pottery for the tourist trade. After 1930 the O'odham made a whiteware that is painted with geometric designs.

The Manuel and Angea families are generally credited with creating modern O'odham pottery. They make a white-based polychrome, but their greatest contribution has been the "Friendship Bowl." Four or more painted hand-holding, dancing figures encircle the outside of the bowl. Facing in, the area under their linked arms and above their waist is usually cut out, creating an open space. The male and female figures dance outside, reminding one and all of our connection with the earth and one another.

Lines of identical linked dancers holding hands are common to ancient Hohokam pottery dating to A.D. 800-1100. They now provide O'odham potters with a great source for ideas. Art and academics combine to create economic development. Annie Manuel

Maricopa, Apache, and Yuman

There are 38 separate tribal-cultural groups in the American Southwest, each with their own unique arts and crafts. Though the Pueblo and Hopi dominate the pottery market, members from other tribes almost unknown to the outside world make pottery worth seeing and collecting.

MARICOPA

The Maricopa make a unique black on burnished redware in a small variety of shapes

Sheldon Nunez-Velarde draws inspiration for his micaceous pottery from the Jicarilla Apache basketmaking tradition. Apache burden baskets characteristically have dangling tas made of leather and the metal from chewing tobacco cans.

including plates, bowls, pitchers, and their signature long-neck vases. Also made are black-on-cream and black-on-cream-and-red vessels. All three styles date back to the earliest record of Maricopa pottery, about 1850.

Maricopa pottery has undergone two revivals. The first occurred in 1937 when government agent Elizabeth Hart encouraged museums to show an interest in Maricopa pottery, thereby motivating potters to produce better quality work. They did, prices went up, and the

Modern museums play an important role in preserving potte traditions that have seemingly died out. The Arizona State Museum owns an extensive collection of Maricopa pottery which can serve as a source of study for those few potters maintaining the tradition. Ida Redbird (front), others unsigne

Apache pottery is similar to the micaceous ware made in Taos and Picuris pueblos. The cultures may have shared clay sources and building techniques. Raw clay is filled with flecks of mica, the silicate mineral that gives the pottery its natural glitter. Believing older pots to be infused with the spirit of their maker, Sheldon Nunez-Velarde keeps a small collection of historic pottery nearby when he works so he can "listen to the advice of my grandmothers."

Pottery from the three Yuman-speaking tribes on the lower Colorado River has all but died out. The tradition includes effigy jars, figurines, and a variety of jars and pots. The School of American Research in Santa Fe is currently sharing its collection with the tribes in an attempt to revive the tradition. Elmer Gates (all)

Maricopa economy improved. When Hart died and World War II broke out, Maricopa pottery was neglected.

A second revival took place in the 1970s. Mary Fernald wrote her anthropology master's thesis on Maricopa pottery by apprenticing to potter Ida Redbird. This union encouraged potters to continue and further explore their art. After another brief period of recognition, Maricopa pottery again slipped into obscurity.

A third revival may be underway. Pottery classes are being taught. Though the temptation to secure a job in Phoenix or the tribal casino is strong, some Maricopas continue to work to ensure Maricopa pottery its deserved day in the sun.

APACHE

Apache pottery resembles Pueblo micaceous ware and has a similar history. Pottery was historically made for use. The Jicarilla of northern New Mexico share the same mountain ranges—hence, some of the same clay sources—as their neighboring Tewa pueblos. Design and forms are similar as well. Overshadowed by the production of baskets and beading, pottery making focuses mainly on utilitarian vessels. Recently a few Apache potters have begun applying cultural symbols to pottery, much like the basket weavers do. With a new-found cultural identity, Apache pottery is an art form with a promising future.

YUMAN

There are three Yuman-speaking tribes living in the southwest corner of Arizona—the Mohave, the Cocopa, and the Yuma—collectively known as the Colorado River Indian Tribes. The red-on-buff pottery that all groups once made resembles the work of their Hohokam ancestors. In the late 1960s, Mohave potters Annie Fields and Elmer Gates were active and brought recognition to area pottery. When they both passed away, so did the tradition. Yuman pottery awaits a rebirth.

Mata Ortiz - Casas Grandes

Mata Ortiz-Casas Grandes pottery is some of the finest art pottery made in the Southwest today. Its quick rise to fame in the densely populated world of Southwest pottery proves that quality and innovation can still find a strong place in the market. The pottery is characterized by its light weight and thin walls. Both the black-on-black and polychrome styles showcase intricate and highly skilled painted designs.

Mata Ortiz pottery rivals Acoma for having the thinnest-walled pots. Potters here have quickly gained technical and artistic excellence. Olga Quezada

The black-on-black technique used on many Mata Ortiz pots was first learned by Juan Quezada during a fortunate meeting with San Ildefonso Pueblo's famous Maria Martinez. A growing number of black pots are really a deep gray, made by coating the clay pot with graphite. Mata Ortiz potters often alter a pot's shape by pushing the sidewalls in or out, like this one, creating what one dealer calls a "meteor" pot. Eduardo Ortiz

The Mata Ortiz tradition is recent. Unlike most other pottery communities, it did not have a functional-ware past, but was founded and continues as fine art. It began with one man following childhood curiosities.

The ancient pueblo of Paquime lies near the town of Mata Ortiz, about 70 miles west of El Paso, in the Mexican state of Chihuahua. Archaeologist Adolph Bandelier explored there in the 1890s, but local Indian inhabitants—who remained uninterested in their ancient history—were mostly ignored. In the 1960s, Juan Quezada, a young Native railroad worker with artistic desires, found Casas Grandes shards and decided to make pottery. Through years of trial and error, he reinvented for himself the entire technique of

Mata Ortiz designs are generally made on an unslipped surface. They are painted with brushes usually made from a few long strands of children's hair. Instead of using the tip, the brush is laid down and pulled through to create a straight line. Curved lines made in this manner take great skill. Once outlined, shapes are filled in with a larger brush. When the painting is completed, the pot is polished one last time before firing. (Top to bottom, left to right) Julio Mora, Jose M. Martinez, Martha M. Quezada, Gerardo Cata G., Jesus Martinez, Martha M. Dominguez, Julio Mora

pottery making. He had to find clay, learn building techniques, discover the need for temper and the effect of paint, and study firing techniques—with little or no help. All of Quezada's efforts were inspired by the shards he found on walks.

His first pieces were crude, unsigned, and sold by traders as prehistoric. When he began signing pieces in paint, the traders would erase his name. Quezada then etched his name in the pot and, with the help of an interested American named Spencer MacCallum, introduced his work to the world. He met Maria Martinez before she died and learned the secrets of black-on-black pottery. A large number of pots are now made using this technique.

While teaching at the Idyllwild School for the Arts, he met Lucy Lewis of Acoma. Impressed by his skill with clay, she is said to have remarked to one of her daughters that Quezada must certainly be descended from the children that Acoma stories say were traded into Mexico by the padres for a new church bell.

Quezada achieved the fame accorded to potters like Nampeyo, Lucy Lewis, and Maria Martinez, introducing a new and independent economy to his poor village.

Family, relatives, and neighboring villages became inspired, accounting for over 300 potters now working. With its very fine craftsmanship, increasing aesthetics, and relatively low cost, Mata Ortiz-Casas Grandes pottery is clearly challenging Pueblo and Hopi pottery for top billing in the pottery market.

Mata Ortiz clay comes in diverse colors and temperaments. The gray clay that fires to a beige color has a natural plasticity that makes it easy to work with. The high iron content of red clay turns it deep black in a reduction fire. The rare white clay is hard, brittle, and difficult to use. Yoly Cedezma, Julio Cedezma, Lazaro Ponce, Tavo Silveito, Gloria Hernandez, Rosa Loya (center)

New Directions

In all culturally generated art forms throughout the world, there arise those individuals whose role becomes that of pushing the creative envelope. No matter how conservative or protective a tribal community may seem, there has always been room for and acceptance of individual artistic expression. Pottery is no exception. By its very tactile and intimate nature, pottery inspires quality and creativity in its makers. Those who truly listen to the clay, listen well to themselves.

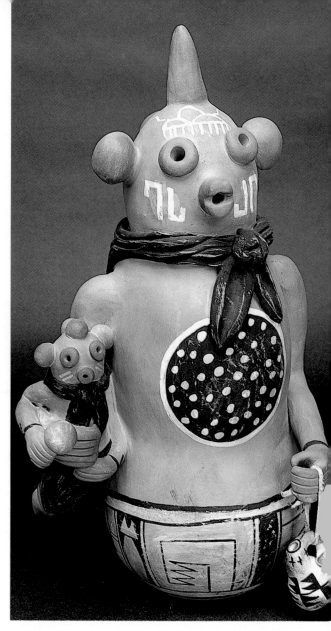

Laguna potter Michael Kanteena's replications of ancient pottery help renew his cultural identity. "Growing up in California, I never knew the Indian religion. Seeing and holding ancient pottery in museums helped me feel the strength of my tradition. Sometimes when I'm working, I feel like I've lived back in that time."

Andrew Harvier responds to his mixed Santa Clara, Taos, and Tohono O'odham heritage to create fine-crafted pottery. A philosophical title and commentary accompany each one. Shown are Ancient Tracks, Heaven's Garden, and Four Winds.

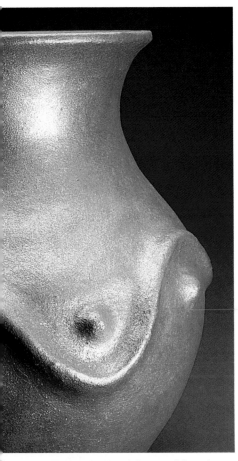

Anthony Durand raised the traditional utilitarian pottery of his native Picuris Pueblo to a fine art. Though their inspiration is functional, the craft and finish make his among the finest micaceous ware being made.

New directions are sometimes bold, but often subtle. Potters such as Rainey Naha, from Hopi, add their own creative twists to traditional symbols, in this case the bird wing or "migration" symbol.

Inspired by Jicarilla Apache basketry, Sheldon Nunez-Velarde has created a unique look with his micaceous ware. The basket-styled plate was actually made using one of his grandmother's yucca baskets as the base. It was necessary to add clay to the rim and interior to give the piece strength. Upon discovering this, Sheldon decided to give the structural supports a cultural pattern. The texture of the original basket is evident on both sides of the pottery. He also enjoys making clay jewelry and functional pots.

Lizards are not only playful—they also have much to teach desert-dwelling people about water use and surviving heat. Acoma potter Ruth B. Paisano chooses to honor them by merging the techniques of appliqué and painting.

Creativity is relative. It can exist to great degrees within a cultural context, but not be perceived by outsiders at all. It can appear wildly abstract to a Euro-American viewer but be conservative by tribal standards, or it can be viewed as being so far from the cultural standard that it is not seen as part of the art form at all. The beauty of all tribal arts is that they can be many things to many people.

By breaking out of a cultural stereotype, Native artists present the viewing public with an education. It is not so much that the art looks Indian, but that the art was made by an Indian. The first is creatively and ultimately patronizing; the latter allows the artist and the viewer to connect as human beings, as equals.

Energetic young potters from Santa Clara Pueblo conduct experiments with multiple firing and design concepts that set new standards for creative excellence. Being "non-traditional" seems to be the tradition! Ron Suazo carves the opening of his multi-hued pots to complement his fine incised designs. Effie Garcia creates blackware with elegant simplicity. Young Forrest Tafoya tries any and all combinations of clay and technique. He created these two natural clay pieces as a student!

Where some artists explore new directions in fine art, others choose to explore the fine art of American and cultural kitsch. The Santa Claus is but one figure created to celebrate Christmas. Nativity scenes are also popular, and potters in numerous communities receive handsome commissions to create them. On the other hand, the Indian in the canoe could either be celebrating or commenting on America's Indian stereotype. Anthony Lovato, Marie Romero, Henrietta Gachupin, Judy Toya (all from Jemez)

The entire village of Mata Ortiz seems to be headed in new directions as artists inspire and compete with each other in an unmatched creative frenzy. Some potters, like Cesar Dominquez, marble their clay. This is not a surface treatment, but three clays carefully mixed and formed. It is a technique seen nowhere else. Others, like Lionel Lopez, create dynamic incised designs or combine multiple techniques and discover new ones in the process. Mata Ortiz is home to a wonderful creative energy.

59

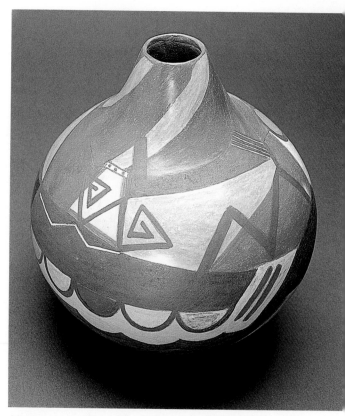

Melon pots have been adopted by many potters. The concept stems from the naturally occurring segment lines found in squash. Jemez potters Laura Gauchapin (top 2) and her nephew Damian Toya enjoy "doing things" with the concept.

Numerous potters have special collectors or mentors who support their work. Rick Dillingham was such a person. He purchased a great number of pots from established and struggling artists and shared with them the fruits of his own talent as an internationally known ceramist. Upon his death Hopi artist Dextra Quotskuyva created this pot to honor their friendship.

Fun is the primary purpose and meaning of this lizard pot by Sharon and Bernard Lewis of Acoma.

Preston Duwyenie merged pottery and jewelry interests in his "Shifting Sands" series. Inundated by the textural quality of the sand dunes around his Hopi village home, he chose to put their pattern into clay. The silver inlay represents the precious quality of desert water.

Today's Southwest potters are exploring new forms, colors, and combinations of designs. Many have begun to paint or carve personal experiences on their pottery, much like a painter with canvas. Others have chosen to experiment with asymmetrical or more figurative forms. Native potters have always felt that making pottery was a means to express both their cultural and personal identity. They are doing it now with much more artistic freedom.

To achieve their vision some artists are out of necessity using commercial clays and paints, but their work remains hand-built with the same integrity as those artists working with hand-dug earth clays.

The work shown here is but a small example of people going beyond the bounds of their chosen medium.

Glen Gomez, of Taos and Pojoaque ancestry, delights in creating micaceous pottery from forms he sees in nature. The pitcher (left) was prompted by gourds and the canteen (right) by the interior of a flower.

The Next Generation

Children's pottery makes a great collection, and it stands on its own creative merits. It is advisable when purchasing adult work to ask if the potter's children have any work for sale. If you do buy and the child is present, have him or her tell you about the piece. Tell the child about yourself and where you're from. Show photos. Not only does it add to the child's education, but it also provides a big dose of self-esteem. In light of the current state of cultural erosion among Indian tribes, your small act may also help maintain cultural continuity. (Photo below) Teresa Pacheco, Rosie Swentzell, Michael Tafoya, Brandon Gonzales, Derek Gonzales, Jeramy Gonzales, KhaPovi Harvier, Celestino Yazza, Wayne Yazza, Jenseda Naranjo

KhaPovi Harvier of Santa Clara Pueblo

Teresa Pacheco from Santo Domingo

Children's pottery can be as interesting and inspiring as that of adults.

Purchase, Collecting, and Care

PURCHASE

Southwestern pottery is a national treasure and one of the most accessible art forms anywhere. The new purchaser of a piece of Southwest pottery is in for an extraordinary experience. Where to begin?

If you love it and know you can't live without it, buy it. Short of instant purchase, it's best to shop around and get a strong idea for variety, quality, and price. The many galleries, shops, and museums that feature pottery are the best places to get an education. A number of good books on the subject can supplement your learning. Reading up on the culture will advance your appreciation of the art and the artist as well. Many potters, especially among the Pueblos and Hopi, own shops in or near their homes. A visit to a pueblo also gives you a feel for the cultural context from which the pottery comes. You can purchase pots from a reputable shop or from the artists themselves, at their home or at one of the many arts and crafts shows sponsored by museums and other agencies across the Southwest and throughout the calendar year.

COLLECTING

Once you make your first purchase, you may get the collector's bug. Buying a few pots is one thing; collecting is a serious passion. Collecting is the conscious gathering of pottery along a particular set of themes. Collections are often: from a single style (such as Navajo or Santa Clara red), of one pottery family (the Jemez family of Marie Romero, for example), all figures, animals (just bears, lizards, or all), only carved or incised (limiting one to only half the available pottery!), children's work (with its own artistic appeal),

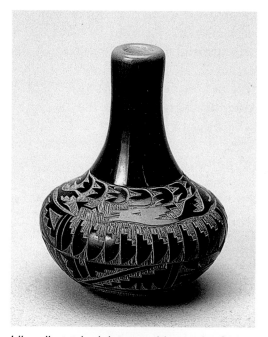

Like all good miniatures, this one by Santa Clara artist Geri Naranjo embodies all the technique and artistry of a full-sized pot.

When you can buy direct from a potter, do so. That is the best way to get the "story behind the scenery." And always remember that collecting is fun! Marie Romero, Jemez

62

miniatures (from one area or everywhere), or some other personally interesting theme.

Collections can range in size and scope from a few pots worth a few hundred dollars to many pots worth many thousands of dollars.

CARE

Once you've purchased a piece of pottery or started a collection, you'll want to take care of it. The level of care given often depends on your intent in buying—and on what you paid for a piece. (There are old Maria Martinez pots purchased for a few dollars, converted to lamps, and still worth several hundred to several thousand dollars today!) Pottery is fragile. It will break when dropped or crack when hit. While pots can be restored, the value cannot.

If you bought it for use, it probably won't last as long as one on display. Micaceous ware is often bought to cook with. Ask the potter their recipe for seasoning a cooking pot.

Even though paint and clay are fused together in the firing process, they are still easily damaged. Set your pottery in a well-protected area. Simon Vallo, Acoma

The paint on the pot above is flaking due to water damage. Unless specifically noted, pottery should not be allowed to hold water as it seeps into the clay and weakens it. The pot below suffers from excessive handling and being placed next to objects that have rubbed against it.

If you buy a piece that will receive repeated handling, you might shy away from any red or black polished ware (Santa Clara, San Ildefonso, Mata Ortiz) as finger oils, smudges, and scratches are not easily removed.

No Southwest pot should hold water unless otherwise specified by the potter. Clay is porous and standing water will seep through the pot, weakening its structure and causing the paint to flake off. Pottery purchased for use as a planter should employ a glass liner.

If you purchase for display, consider the presentation. Many people create special pottery niches in their architecture, allowing the work open space in which to "breathe." It can be fun occasionally rearranging your collection to a new composition or to accept a new acquisition. Simple backgrounds usually show off the pottery best.

To keep a pot from marring furniture or from losing the artist's signature, place the pot on a felt or buckskin pad.

Dust with a light touch using a clean, dry, soft cloth or feather duster.

Your pottery purchase places you among the thousands of people who have found the good spirit of the Southwest in a piece of pottery. Indian potters believe that by taking care of a pot, it and the spirits contained within it will take care of you and your family for years to come.

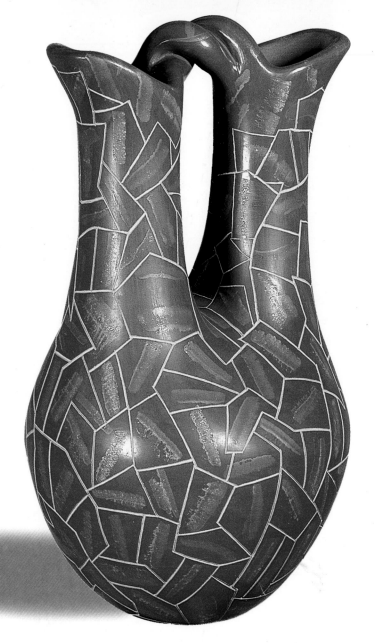

*"Pieces of Love" reflects Santa Clara
artist Andrew Harvier's feeling for life.
"Like this pot, life is a series of pieces
that fit magically together."*

SUGGESTED READING

BAHTI, MARK. *Pueblo Stories & Storytellers.* Tucson, Arizona: Treasure Chest Publications, 1996.

BAHTI, MARK. *Southwestern Indian Arts & Crafts.* Las Vegas, Nevada: KC Publications, 1997 (rev. ed.).

BUNZEL, RUTH L. *The Pueblo Potter: A Study of Creative Imagination in Primitive Art.* New York: Dover Publications, Inc., 1929.

DILLINGHAM, RICK. *Acoma & Laguna Pottery.* Santa Fe, New Mexico: School of American Research Press, 1992.

DILLINGHAM, RICK. *Fourteen Families in Pueblo Pottery.* Albuquerque: University of New Mexico Press, 1994.

EATON, LINDA B. "Tradition and Innovation: The Pottery of New Mexico's Pueblos," *Plateau Magazine*, Vol. 6, No. 3. Flagstaff, Arizona: Museum of Northern Arizona, 1990.

GAULT, RAMONA. *Artistry in Clay: A Buyer's Guide to Southwestern Indian Pottery.* Santa Fe, New Mexico: Southwestern Association for Indian Arts, 1991.

HARTMAN, RUSSELL P., and JAN MUSIAL. *Navajo Pottery: Traditions & Innovations.* Flagstaff, Arizona: Northland Publishing, 1987.

HAYES, ALLAN, and JOHN BLOM. *Southwestern Pottery: Anasazi to Zuni.* Flagstaff, Arizona: Northland Publishing, 1996.

HUCKO, BRUCE. *Where There Is No Name for Art: The Art of Tewa Pueblo Children.* Santa Fe, New Mexico: School of American Research Press, 1996.

PARKS, WALTER P. *The Miracle of Mata Ortiz: Juan Quezada and the Potters of Northern Chihuahua.* Riverside, California: The Coulter Press, 1993.

PETERSON, SUSAN. *Pottery by American Indian Women: The Legacy of Generations.* Washington, D.C.: The National Museum of Women in the Arts, 1997.

RODEE, MARIAN, and JAMES OSTLER. *Zuni Pottery.* Atglen, Pennsylvania: Schiffer Publishing, Ltd., 1986.

STOEPPELMANN, JANET, and MARY FERNALD. *Dirt for Making Things: An Apprenticeship in Maricopa Pottery.* Flagstaff, Arizona: Northland Publishing, 1995.

SWENTZELL, RINA. *Children of Clay: A Family of Pueblo Potters.* Minneapolis, Minnesota: First Avenue Editions, 1992.

TRIMBLE, STEPHEN. *Talking with the Clay: The Art of Pueblo Pottery.* Santa Fe, New Mexico: School of American Research Press, 1987.

Books on Indian Culture and the Southwest: Southwestern Indian Arts and Crafts, Southwestern Indian Tribes, Southwestern Indian Ceremonials, Southwestern Indian Pottery, Canyon de Chelly, Monument Valley, Mesa Verde, Grand Circle Adventure, The Rocks Begin to Speak, The Southern Paiutes, The Navajo Treaty, Zuni Fetishes, Zuni Fetishes Expanded Edition. A hardbound edition combining the first 3 Southwestern Indian books is also available.

Other Series by KC Publications:
   The Story Behind the Scenery - on America's national parks.
   in pictures - companion series on America's national parks.
   • **Translation Packages available.**
   Voyage of Discovery - on the expansion of the western United States.
NEW! WildLife @ Yellowstone.

To receive our catalog with over 115 titles:

Call (800-626-9673), fax (702-433-3420), write to the address below,
   Or visit our web site at www.kcpublications.com

Published by KC Publications, 3245 E. Patrick Ln., Suite A, Las Vegas, NV 89120.

*Inside back cover: The skilled hands
of Jemez potter Marie Romero
give final form to a wedding vase*

*Back cover: Southwestern Indian
pottery brings a living beauty
to the lives of both the creator
and the collector*

Created, Designed, and Published in the
Ink formulated by Daihan Ink Co
Color separations & printing by Doosan Corporation, Seoul,
Paper produced exclusively by Hankuk Paper Mfg. Co